Tests

AFRICAN AMERICAN LITERATURE

Voices in a Tradition

HOLT, RINEHART AND WINSTON
Harcourt Brace & Company

Austin • New York • Orlando • Atlanta • San Francisco • Boston • Dallas • Toronto • London

STAFF CREDITS

EDITORIAL

Project Director:
Fannie Safier

Managing Editor:
Richard Sime

Senior Book Editor:
Laura Baci

Editorial Staff:
Daniela Guggenheim, Bobbi Hernandez, Marc Ottaviani

Editorial Support:
Mark Koenig

PRODUCTION AND DESIGN

Director:
Athena Blackorby

Art Director:
Betty Mintz

Photo Research:
Mary Monaco

Production Support:
Shoshana Rothaizer

Electronic Publishing:
Carol Martin, *Electronic Publishing Manager;* Kristy Sprott, *Project Manager;* Rina May Ouellette, Michele Ruschhaupt, Ethan Thompson, *Electronic Publishing Team*

Cover: *The Lovers (Somali Friends)* by Loïs Mailou Jones, casein on canvas, 1950.
Courtesy of The Estate of Thurlow E. Tibbs, Jr.

Printed in the United States of America

ISBN 0-03-051998-5

1 2 3 4 5 054 00 99 98 97

A Note to the Teacher

This test booklet accompanies *African American Literature: Voices in a Tradition.* It includes individual tests for unit introductions and major selections in the anthology as well as tests for groups of short selections. Many of these tests have three sections. The first is usually a test of reading comprehension dealing with basic understanding and literary techniques. The second is generally a vocabulary test. The third section is an essay test.

This test booklet also contains analogy tests, in which the vocabulary items are drawn from selections in the textbook. At the back of the booklet are tests for review and mastery.

The reading comprehension tests beginning on page 169 focus on items that appear on standardized tests. These tests, intended for practice, contain hints and self-check answer keys. Also included is a proficiency test based on thematically related selections.

Some individual tests are intended to be given as open-book tests; others, if you wish, may also be used in that way. All objective tests are multiple choice or matching column. Each has 100 as the best possible score. Essay tests may be graded separately.

Answers to each test are printed on pages 352–355 of the *Teacher's Manual.*

Table of Contents

Unit Four
RECONSTRUCTION TO RENAISSANCE

Unit Five
THE HARLEM RENAISSANCE

Unit Six
FROM RENAISSANCE TO MID-FORTIES

PASSAGES

Toni Cade Bambara

Raymond's Run

Unit One

Text page 4

A. Understanding Main Ideas

Write the letter of the best answer to each question. (10 points each)

1. Who is the only person in the neighborhood that Squeaky admits can run faster than she does?
   a. Raymond   **b.** George   **c.** her father   **d.** Mary Louise

   1. _____

2. Which of these words best describes Squeaky?
   a. shy   **c.** snobbish
   b. mean   **d.** self-confident

   2. _____

3. Which of the following phrases best describes Gretchen?
   a. Squeaky's classmate   **c.** an old friend
   b. a rival   **d.** a pianist

   3. _____

4. What is Squeaky's major responsibility?
   a. helping to clean the house
   b. practicing piano
   c. earning money for clothes
   d. taking care of an older child

   4. _____

5. Which of these names is another nickname for Squeaky?
   a. Mercury   **b.** Beanstalk   **c.** Skinny   **d.** May Pole

   5. _____

B. Vocabulary

Each of the following sentences contains an italicized word that appears in the selection. Choose the best synonym for each italicized word. (10 points each)

6. Squeaky considers Cynthia a *prodigy*.
   a. showoff   **c.** spoiled brat
   b. gifted child   **d.** phony

   6. _____

7. Squeaky once wore a dress made of *organdy*.
   a. woolen cloth   **c.** shiny nylon
   b. fine silk   **d.** sheer cotton

   7. _____

8. In a school *pageant* Squeaky played the role of a strawberry.
   a. dramatic performance   c. carnival
   b. parade   d. assembly program   8. _____

9. Some of the children in the park were *rowdy*.
   a. lost   b. irritable   c. disorderly   d. tearful   9. _____

10. The runners *crouch* over the get ready mark.
    a. lean forward   c. bend low
    b. crowd together   d. leap   10. _____

C. Essay

Choose one of the following topics for a one-paragraph essay. You can refer to the story as often as you wish.

1. Is Squeaky a believable character? Does she act and speak the way a real person in her circumstances would behave? In answering, give at least **3** different kinds of evidence from the story.

2. Tell what Squeaky means by "real" and "phony" people. Then decide which people in the story would belong in the *real* category and which in the *phony*, and give your reasons.

Ted Poston
The Revolt of the Evil Fairies

Text page 23

A. Understanding Main Ideas

Write the letter of the best answer to each question. (10 points each)

1. Which of the following statements is *not* correct?
   a. The school play was presented at the opera house.
   b. The presentation never changed.
   c. White spectators sat in the front rows.
   d. Parts were assigned between Christmas and February.

   1. _____

2. Roger's main qualification for playing the male lead was
   a. his father's political connections
   b. his popularity
   c. making the best grades in the class
   d. the color of his skin

   2. _____

3. The narrator wanted the role of Prince Charming chiefly because
   a. he was tired of playing the Head Evil Fairy
   b. he was in love with the leading lady
   c. he liked to impress his teachers
   d. Sarah was to play the Head Good Fairy

   3. _____

4. What unexpected action occurred during the second act?
   a. Prince Charming struck the Head Evil Fairy with his sword.
   b. The Head Evil Fairy cast a spell on Sleeping Beauty.
   c. The Head Evil Fairy drew a sword against Prince Charming.
   d. The Good Fairies and the Evil Fairies began to fight.

   4. _____

5. Which of the following did *not* occur during the final act?
   a. Sleeping Beauty awoke and ran offstage.
   b. Leonardius began screaming hysterically.
   c. Rat Joiner settled old scores.
   d. The curtain rang down.

   5. _____

B. Vocabulary

Each of the following sentences contains an italicized word that appears in the selection. Choose the best synonym for each italicized word. (10 points each)

6. The local undertaker *invariably* took the same seat.
   a. never
   b. seldom
   c. without fail
   d. often

   6. _____

7. The *prominent* citizens sat in the front rows.
   a. widely known
   b. wealthy
   c. senior
   d. well-dressed

   7. _____

8. The Head Evil Fairy was expected to *skulk* back in the shadows.
   a. stalk
   b. hide
   c. tremble
   d. move stealthily

   8. _____

9. The narrator wrote *fervent* love letters.
   a. silly   b. lengthy   c. elaborate   d. emotional

   9. _____

10. The Head Evil Fairy was expected to *expire* in the final act.
    a. give up
    b. die
    c. ask for forgiveness
    d. retire

    10. _____

C. Essay

Choose one of the following topics for a one-paragraph essay. You can refer to the story as often as you wish.

1. Discuss the elements of discrimination that existed within the black community of Hopkinsville and show the effects on the children in the school play.

2. The narrator claims that striking Leonardius was a "case of self-defense." Do you agree or do you think he had other motives? Defend your answer with specific evidence from the story.

Maya Angelou
from **I Know Why the Caged Bird Sings**   Text page 33

A. Understanding Main Ideas

Write the letter of the best answer to each question. (10 points each)

1. Marguerite and Bailey were sent to Arkansas because
   a. their grandmother needed help running the Store
   b. their parents wanted them to see new places
   c. their parents' marriage broke up
   d. their grandmother was sick and wanted to see the children   1. _____

2. Returning to the Store in the afternoon, the workers
   a. were cheerful and happy that the workday was over
   b. relaxed over a supper of crackers and sardines
   c. divided the money they had earned during the day
   d. were tired and grumbled over their insufficient wages   2. _____

3. For Marguerite, working in the Store
   a. was a kind of adventure
   b. made her angry and resentful
   c. was confusing and difficult
   d. interfered with her schoolwork   3. _____

4. On Sunday mornings Momma
   a. let Marguerite and Bailey sleep until she returned from church
   b. took the children for a ride through the country
   c. fixed the children a quick breakfast and then left for church
   d. served a breakfast that was to keep the children quiet until afternoon   4. _____

5. Of the many values Marguerite learned from her grandmother, the most
   influential one was
   a. respect for strangers
   b. the satisfaction gained from hard work
   c. the joy of reading
   d. the importance of money   5. _____

B. Vocabulary

Each of the following sentences contains an italicized word that appears in the selection. Choose the best synonym for each italicized word. (10 points each)

6. Momma had a *mobile* lunch counter.
   a. busy   b. temporary   c. moveable   d. small

   6. _____

7. Marguerite *winced* when she pictured the workers repairing their sacks.
   a. flinched   b. grinned   c. groaned   d. cried

   7. _____

8. She *persistently* punished herself for errors in judgment.
   a. occasionally   c. stubbornly
   b. quietly   d. repeatedly

   8. _____

9. Marguerite felt she was stretched between *loathing* Reverend Thomas' voice and wanting to listen to the sermon.
   a. hating   b. loving   c. admiring   d. enjoying

   9. _____

10. *Pandemonium* spread through the church.
    a. silence   b. disorder   c. laughter   d. happiness

    10. _____

C. Essay

Choose one of the following topics for a one-paragraph essay. You can refer to the selection as often as you like.

1. How does Maya Angelou show that as a child she was a careful observer of people and places? Refer to specific evidence in the selection.

2. Maya Angelou writes about living through the Great Depression of the 1930s. What do you learn about this period from her narrative? In what way does her autobiography help to give us a vivid picture of the past?

Merle Hodge
from **Crick Crack, Monkey**

Text page 48

A. Understanding Main Ideas

Write the letter of the best answer to each question. (10 points each)

1. Which of these features was part of Sir's regular performance?
   a. He whispered so that the children had to strain to hear his voice.
   b. He called the attendance roll.
   c. He paced back and forth, tapping a whip against his leg.
   d. He distributed paper and pencils to each child.

   1. _____

2. How did Sir correct the children's errors in penmanship?
   a. He kept them after school to practice their writing.
   b. He punished them with his whip.
   c. He held up examples of model writing.
   d. He assigned extra homework.

   2. _____

3. Which of these statements most accurately describes the children's reactions to Sir?
   a. They were frightened of him and confused by his methods.
   b. They were amused by his performance.
   c. Although he was strict, they knew they were learning a great deal.
   d. Once they got used to him, they admired and respected him.

   3. _____

4. When visitors came to class, Sir did all of the following *except*
   a. ask students to recite
   b. smile at the class
   c. put away his whip
   d. tell the children to rise

   4. _____

5. Sir continually drilled the class
   a. in multiplication tables
   b. in reading aloud
   c. in rising from their seats quietly
   d. in memorizing famous quotations

   5. _____

B. Vocabulary

Each of the following sentences contains an italicized word that appears in the selection. Choose the best synonym for each italicized word. (10 points each)

6. Sir often spoke to the class at length about such subjects as *veracity*.
   a. truthfulness
   b. accuracy
   c. the scientific method
   d. insolence

   6. _____

7. Copying out the row of words at the top of the blackboard did not add to any student's *enlightenment*.
   a. skill in penmanship
   b. understanding and knowledge
   c. self-discipline
   d. improvement in spelling

   7. _____

8. Sir read the class stories about *steeds*.
   a. famous heroes
   b. foreign places
   c. reluctant learners
   d. spirited horses

   8. _____

9. On occasion, Sir *relinquished* his whip.
   a. studied
   b. let go
   c. handed over
   d. lowered

   9. _____

10. Silence in Sir's classroom was *unaccountable*.
    a. rewarding
    b. disturbing
    c. without explanation
    d. restful

    10. _____

C. Essay

Write an essay on the following topic. Refer to the selection as necessary.

Imagine that you, as narrator, are writing a letter to relatives in the United States, giving your impressions of Sir. Include a physical description as well as a description of his regular performances. Write naturally.

Peter Abrahams
from **Tell Freedom**

Text page 55

A. Understanding Main Ideas

Write the letter of the best answer to each question. (10 points each)

1. During the long walk to the pig farm, the boys pass the time
   a. teasing dogs
   b. racing and pitching stones
   c. eating bread
   d. singing songs

   1. _____

2. At the pig farm, the narrator angers a white man because
   a. he forgets to pay for the crackling
   b. he refuses to look at the man
   c. he holds up the line
   d. he does not address the man in the expected way

   2. _____

3. When the white boys appear on the road, Andries advises the narrator to
   a. slow down until the others pass
   b. walk faster
   c. defend himself
   d. pelt them with stones

   3. _____

4. In trying to protect Lee, Uncle Sam uses all of the following excuses
   except one. Which is the exception?
   a. He says the boy is sorry.
   b. He claims to have already punished him.
   c. He says that the boy doesn't know any better.
   d. He admits that the boy's father believes in equality.

   4. _____

5. After the beating
   a. the narrator refuses to apologize
   b. Uncle Sam begins to cry
   c. Uncle Sam explains his reasons for the beating
   d. Aunt Liza brings the boy sweets

   5. _____

B. Vocabulary

Each of the following sentences contains an italicized word that appears in the selection. Choose the best synonym for each italicized word. (10 points each)

6. Andries's mother spoke in a *plaintive* voice.
   a. loud   **b.** complaining   **c.** quiet   **d.** mournful

   6. _____

7. The narrator wished to avoid the *mockery* in the man's eyes.
   a. challenge   **c.** ridicule
   b. coldness   **d.** humor

   7. _____

8. When he was told about the fight, the narrator's uncle became *remote*.
   a. distant   **b.** frightened   **c.** annoyed   **d.** suspicious

   8. _____

9. During the evening the narrator became *apprehensive*.
   a. uneasy   **b.** stubborn   **c.** impudent   **d.** sorry

   9. _____

10. He lay on the floor *whimpering*.
    a. complaining   **b.** whining   **c.** sleeping   **d.** bellowing

    10. _____

C. Essay

Choose one of the following topics for a one-paragraph essay. You can refer to the story as often as you wish.

1. Although the narrator is the central figure in this selection, the other characters also help us understand how apartheid affects individuals and families. Consider the roles played by Andries, Uncle Sam, and Aunt Liza. How does each one respond to the conflicts in this selection?

2. Discuss the element of setting in this selection. What details does the author include to give you a sense of the land and the people? Refer to specific evidence in your essay.

Analogy Test 1

Recognizing Relationships in Verbal Analogies

Verbal analogies test your understanding of the relationships among words. Look at the following example:

toe : foot :: finger : _____
- **a.** arm
- **b.** hand
- **c.** ring
- **d.** nail

The correct answer is **b.** *Toe* is related to *foot* as *finger* is related to *hand*.

The following analogy questions are based on vocabulary words taken from the selections in Unit One. Choose the letter of the best answer to each question. (10 points each)

1. rowdy : disorderly :: cloddish : _____
- **a.** confused
- **b.** impudent
- **c.** severe
- **d.** ignorant

1. _____

2. calamitous : disastrous :: affluent : _____
- **a.** wealthy
- **b.** different
- **c.** influential
- **d.** insulting

2. _____

3. wayward : obedient :: valiant : _____
- **a.** sparse
- **b.** remote
- **c.** cowardly
- **d.** fervent

3. _____

4. exotic : ordinary :: immobile : _____
- **a.** motionless
- **b.** mobile
- **c.** anxious
- **d.** extraordinary

4. _____

5. fiscal : crisis :: plaintive : _____
- **a.** sadness
- **b.** tune
- **c.** haste
- **d.** disciple

5. _____

6. hound : victim :: reaffirm : _____
- **a.** intentions
- **b.** trek
- **c.** wrath
- **d.** vittles

6. _____

7. relinquish : throne :: dispense : _____
- **a.** upstartedness
- **b.** paranoia
- **c.** justice
- **d.** pandemonium

7. _____

8. persistently : instinctively :: malevolent : _____
   a. quicksilver
   b. invariably
   c. wince
   d. apprehensive

9. inscription : description :: declaimed : _____
   a. declaration
   b. infused
   c. exclaimed
   d. speech

10. prodigy : child :: act : _____
    a. thong
    b. ventriloquist
    c. obsession
    d. flicker

THE AFRICAN LITERARY TRADITION
The Literature of Ancient Egypt

Unit Two

Text pages 76–82

A. Understanding Background

Choose the letter of the best answer to each question. (10 points each)

1. People in the ancient lands of Sumeria and Mesopotamia had a form of writing called
   a. hieratic
   b. hieroglyphic
   c. cuneiform
   d. demotic

   1. _____

2. Early forms of writing appeared on all of the following *except*
   a. clay blocks
   b. papyrus rolls
   c. stone
   d. pulp from rags

   2. _____

3. Pictographic writing
   a. used printed letters
   b. used symbols that looked like objects
   c. had a few simple strokes
   d. was a form of shorthand

   3. _____

4. The chief responsibility of Egyptian scribes was
   a. to interpret sacred writings
   b. to inscribe writings on the walls of tombs
   c. to copy texts
   d. to be skillful orators

   4. _____

5. The Egyptian god who supposedly invented writing was
   a. Thoth   **b.** Osiris   **c.** Aton   **d.** Amon

   5. _____

6. The Pyramid Texts
   a. were inscribed on the tombs of kings
   b. were instructions in the form of proverbs
   c. were inscribed on the inside of stone coffins
   d. were written on papyrus rolls

   6. _____

7. Egyptian religious literature included all of the following *except*
   a. spells
   b. autobiography
   c. hymns
   d. incantations

   7. _____

B. Interpreting Literature

Choose the letter of the best answer to each question. (10 points each)

8. In "The Hymn to the Aton," Aton is identified with
   a. Egypt   c. darkness
   b. Akhenaton   d. Re   8. _____

9. "The Hymn to the Aton" is best described as
   a. a song in praise of a god
   b. a prayer for forgiveness
   c. a poem honoring the rulers of Egypt
   d. a tribute to the pharaoh   9. _____

10. The Aton is given credit for all of the following *except*
    a. bringing beauty to the land
    b. driving away darkness
    c. creating the world
    d. assuming the form of a human being   10. _____

The Oral Tradition

Text pages 83–96

Understanding Background and Literature

Choose the letter of the best answer to each question. (10 points each)

1. Which of the following statements is *not* accurate?
   a. Arabic language and alphabet were introduced into Africa during the nineteenth century.
   b. European missionaries used the Latin alphabet to record African languages.
   c. European languages spread in Africa as a result of exploration and colonization.
   d. The literature written in native African languages at first served a religious purpose.

   1. _____

2. Which of the following statements is *not* a true description of the oral tradition?
   a. Most literature in modern Africa is oral.
   b. The spread of literacy has replaced the oral tradition in most African countries.
   c. Storytellers are important members of African communities.
   d. Stories are usually told at night.

   2. _____

3. Call-and-response refers to
   a. the exchange of riddles
   b. the satirizing of social misbehavior
   c. the interaction between a storyteller and audience
   d. the recitation of poems and tales

   3. _____

4. Storytelling includes all of the following *except*
   a. song   c. mime
   b. dance contests d. drums

   4. _____

5. In contemporary Africa, griots tend to be
   a. interpreters of languages
   b. preservers of ancient traditions
   c. strolling players
   d. professional musicians

   5. _____

6. The two main functions of tribal poets are praise-singing and
   a. reading fortunes
   b. satire
   c. avenging wrongs
   d. telling riddles

6. _____

7. The *nanga* is
   a. a musical instrument
   b. a form of call-and-response
   c. a praise song
   d. a tale of injustice

7. _____

8. What is the chief threat to the preservation of the oral tradition in Africa?
   a. Oral performers are hated and feared by those in power.
   b. Modern media are reducing direct contact between performers and their audiences.
   c. Storytelling interferes with the workday.
   d. Many oral performers have been jailed or sent into exile.

8. _____

9. Which of the following is *not* a characteristic of proverbs?
   a. They express wisdom or common sense.
   b. They are brief.
   c. They are passed on from generation to generation.
   d. They cannot be translated.

9. _____

10. Proverbs are most like
    a. nursery rhymes
    b. Egyptian instructions
    c. the morals in fables
    d. anecdotes

10. _____

Folk Tales

Understanding Background and Literature

Choose the letter of the best answer to each question. (10 points each)

1. The animal characters in African folk tales include all of the following *except*
   a. Ananse the Spider
   b. Brer Rabbit
   c. Tortoise
   d. Monkey

   1. _____

2. The central figure in Caribbean folklore is
   a. Hare   b. Spider   c. Monkey   d. Elephant

   2. _____

3. Among the Yoruba, the folk tale has several parts, including all of the following *except*
   a. a riddling section
   b. a dialogue between narrator and audience
   c. one or two songs
   d. a choral ending

   3. _____

4. Which of the following is *not* a trickster hero?
   a. Brer Rabbit
   b. Ananse
   c. Osebo
   d. Signifying Monkey

   4. _____

5. Which of the following characters is *not* identified correctly?
   a. Osebo—leopard
   b. Ananse—Spider
   c. Oluigbo—king of the bush
   d. Fara Maka—hippopotamus

   5. _____

6. In "Nana Miriam,"
   a. a monster devours crops and brings famine to a tribe
   b. the heroine is ugly
   c. a hippopotamus is defeated by a hunter
   d. the River Niger overflows its banks and kills the monster

   6. _____

7. Why does Nyame want the drum of Osebo?
   a. Osebo had promised it as a gift.
   b. It has magical powers.
   c. He cannot afford to have one made.
   d. He wishes to use it for a ceremony.

   7. _____

8. "Olode the Hunter" can best be described as
   a. a creation myth
   b. a morality tale
   c. a conflict between age and youth
   d. a story of revenge   8. _____

9. Which of these is an example of metamorphosis?
   a. Spider disguises himself as a bird.
   b. A hunter receives fine new clothing.
   c. A leopard is burned by a fire.
   d. A hippopotamus changes into a river.   9. _____

10. Which of these tales explains why stories are told about Ananse?
    a. "Spider's Bargain with God"
    b. "Olode the Hunter"
    c. "Osebo's Drum"
    d. "Nana Miriam"   10. _____

The Epic in Africa

Text pages 118–125

A. Understanding Background

Choose the letter of the best answer to each question. (10 points each)

1. Which of the following statements is *not* an accurate description of the epic?
   a. An epic is a long narrative poem.
   b. An epic deals with the adventures of a heroic figure.
   c. All epics recount true historical events.
   d. An epic can exist in different versions.

   1. _____

2. The best-known African epic
   a. tells about the founder of the Empire of Mali
   b. gives the history of the ruler of the Songhay Empire
   c. deals with the founder of the Zulu Empire
   d. fuses the traditions of the *Iliad* and the *Odyssey*

   2. _____

3. The chief purpose of the African epic was
   a. to entertain the king and his courtiers
   b. to teach children to obey their elders
   c. to distinguish between history and legend
   d. to serve as models of behavior

   3. _____

B. Interpreting Literature

Choose the letter of the best answer to each question. (10 points each)

4. The griot gives various reasons for his importance. Which of the following is *not* one of them?
   a. He knows many old secrets.
   b. He can use magic against an enemy.
   c. He teaches kings about their ancestors.
   d. He helps to settle disputes between tribes.

   4. _____

5. Sundiata is known by various names, but *not* as
   a. the son of the Buffalo
   b. the son of the Lion
   c. Sogolon-Djata
   d. Sosso the Magnificent

   5. _____

6. Sundiata's enemy is
   a. Soumaoro
   b. Balla Fasséké
   c. the king of the Bobos
   d. Alexander the Great

   6. _____

7. How do the warring kings declare their grievances?
   a. Each sends an embassy to explain why he is waging war.
   b. They carry on a dialogue through mental telepathy.
   c. Each one sends a bird to deliver his words.
   d. They exchange griots.

   7. _____

8. Which of the following is *not* one of the strategies used by Sundiata to capture Sosso?
   a. He positions his main army outside the city gate.
   b. His soldiers use ladders to scale the wall of the city.
   c. He rains stones down on enemy soldiers.
   d. His archers fire flaming arrows over the ramparts of the city.

   8. _____

9. In the magic chamber, Sundiata finds all of the following *except*
   a. a snake in a pitcher
   b. fetishes
   c. dying owls
   d. a fatal arrow

   9. _____

10. Balla Fasséké is
    a. Soumaoro's servant
    b. Sundiata's griot
    c. a general in Sundiata's army
    d. a sorcerer

    10. _____

THE BEGINNINGS OF
AFRICAN AMERICAN LITERATURE
Introduction

Unit Three

Text page 133

Understanding Main Ideas

Write the letter of the best answer to each question. (10 points each)

1. How was slavery in the New World different from slavery that had existed in the ancient world and in Africa?
   a. Once people were enslaved in the Americas, they could never become free.
   b. For the first time in history, entire families were sold into slavery.
   c. Slavery was now considered the natural condition for certain races of people.
   d. Only in the New World were slaves considered the property of their owners.

   1. _____

2. How were indentured servants different from slaves?
   a. Indentured servants were free to choose their own masters.
   b. After working for a specified time, indentured servants could become free.
   c. Indentured servants received special privileges.
   d. Indentured servants lived in the same households as their masters.

   2. _____

3. How did early black writers try to change the attitudes of white Americans toward the institution of slavery?
   a. They argued that Christianity was opposed to slavery.
   b. They claimed that slavery was contrary to the economic well-being of the nation.
   c. They challenged the legality of slavery.
   d. They urged white Americans to accept the religious and cultural beliefs of Africans.

   3. _____

4. Which of these statements is *not* accurate?
   a. At the opening of the nineteenth century, African Americans comprised about a fifth of the United States population.
   b. People in the North opposed introducing slavery into the original thirteen colonies.
   c. Congress tried to keep the power of slave states and free states balanced.
   d. William Lloyd Garrison was a leader in the antislavery movement.

   4. _____

5. The Underground Railroad can best be described as
   a. a freedom train that ran through an underground tunnel
   b. a campaign of resistance by journalists and ex-slaves
   c. an organization that helped runaway slaves escape to freedom
   d. a network of spies to recapture fugitive slaves

   5. _____

6. Who was known as the "Moses of her people"?
   a. Phillis Wheatley   c. Harriet Jacobs
   b. Sojourner Truth   d. Harriet Tubman

   6. _____

7. Which of these statements is *not* accurate?
   a. William Wells Brown wrote the first black American novel and
      published the first African American play.
   b. Benjamin Banneker issued a series of almanacs.
   c. The first African American women's fiction was by Sojourner Truth.
   d. The period of the 1850s is sometimes referred to as the first African
      American renaissance.

   7. _____

8. Which event signaled the beginning of the Civil War?
   a. Lincoln's election to the presidency
   b. The Southern bombardment of Fort Sumter
   c. The capture and occupation of Jacksonville, Florida
   d. The issuing of the Emancipation Proclamation

   8. _____

9. What role did African Americans play during the Civil War?
   a. They were never allowed to fight.
   b. They refused to serve in the army.
   c. They served in both the Union army and navy.
   d. They hired out as mercenaries.

   9. _____

10. Slavery was legally abolished in the United States
    a. when African Americans began to desert plantations in the South
    b. when Lincoln signed the Emancipation Proclamation
    c. when Lee surrendered to Grant at Appomattox
    d. when the Thirteenth Amendment to the Constitution was ratified

    10. _____

Olaudah Equiano
from **The Interesting Narrative of the Life of Olaudah Equiano**

Text page 146

A. Understanding Main Ideas

Write the letter of the best answer to each question. (10 points each)

1. How did the narrator and his playmates try to avoid being kidnapped?
   a. Some children acted as lookouts.
   b. The children stayed with adults at all times.
   c. The children played indoors.
   d. The children hid from strangers by climbing trees.

   1. _____

2. The narrator experiences brief happiness when he is reunited with his
   a. friends   b. parents   c. sister   d. second master

   2. _____

3. How old is the narrator when he is forced into slavery?
   a. seven   b. nine   c. eleven   d. fourteen

   3. _____

4. The narrator believes that many things he doesn't understand are caused by
   a. God   c. the white men
   b. magic   d. escaped slaves

   4. _____

5. The slave ship takes its cargo to
   a. a Caribbean island   c. a seaport in Virginia
   b. a South American plantation d. an English village

   5. _____

B. Vocabulary

Each of the following sentences contains an italicized word that appears in the selection. Choose the best synonym for each italicized word. (10 points each)

6. The narrator is reluctant to *trespass* on the reader's patience.
   a. intrude   b. rely   c. comment   d. work

   6. _____

7. The languages of the African captives were not so *copious* as those of the Europeans.
   a. interesting   **b.** simple   **c.** wordy   **d.** complex

7. _____

8. The narrator found his pain *redoubled* after separation from his sister.
   a. intensified   **c.** diminished
   b. restored   **d.** unbearable

8. _____

9. Some slaves were able to *alleviate* their seasickness by remaining on deck.
   a. cure   **b.** delay   **c.** relieve   **d.** forget

9. _____

10. The conditions below deck were *pestilential*.
   a. uncomfortable   **c.** deadly
   b. unsanitary   **d.** irritating

10. _____

C. Essay

Choose one of the following topics for a brief essay. Refer to the selection as often as necessary.

1. Discuss the details Equiano uses to describe his experience on the slave ship. What is the overall effect of his description? Does the author succeed in making you feel what it was like to be on such a ship?

2. What impression do you get of Equiano from his recollections of the past and his comments on his experiences? Write an analysis of the selection in which you focus on the character of the narrator.

Benjamin Banneker
from Letter to Thomas Jefferson

Text page 159

A. Understanding Main Ideas

Write the letter of the best answer to each question. (10 points each)

1. Which of the following statements is true?
   a. At the time of this letter, Jefferson had just been elected President of the United States.
   b. Banneker was freeborn.
   c. Banneker and Jefferson had once been friends.
   d. Jefferson had recently freed his own slaves.   1. _____

2. Banneker asks Jefferson
   a. to create jobs for African Americans
   b. to provide a homeland in Africa for emancipated slaves
   c. to amend the Constitution
   d. to work for the freedom of all people   2. _____

3. The tone of this letter might best be described as
   a. bitterly ironic   c. submissive and humble
   b. serious and calm   d. highly emotional   3. _____

4. In his letter Banneker alludes to all of the following *except*
   a. the Bible
   b. the Declaration of Independence
   c. the Bill of Rights
   d. the Revolutionary War   4. _____

5. Banneker relates the struggle to abolish slavery to
   a. the American Revolution
   b. the Civil War
   c. the Boston Tea Party
   d. the Exodus from Egypt   5. _____

B. Vocabulary

Each of the following sentences contains an italicized word that appears in the selection. Choose the best synonym for each italicized word. (10 points each)

6. Banneker apologizes for his boldness in writing to someone in Jefferson's *station*.
   a. government   **b.** rank   **c.** mood   **d.** state

   6. _____

7. Many people in Banneker's day believed that African Americans did not possess the same mental *endowments* as white people.
   a. creative powers   **c.** feelings and sensations
   b. attitudes   **d.** natural abilities

   7. _____

8. Banneker asks Jefferson to help *eradicate* slavery.
   a. criticize   **c.** wipe out
   b. reduce   **d.** battle

   8. _____

9. Banneker argues that slavery reduces human beings to a state of *degradation*.
   a. humiliation   **b.** horror   **c.** abuse   **d.** dependency

   9. _____

10. Jefferson *professed* to detest oppression.
    a. appeared   **b.** refused   **c.** claimed   **d.** admitted

    10. _____

C. Essay

Write an essay on the following topic. Refer to the selection as often as necessary.

At the beginning of his letter, Banneker refers to the widely held belief that African Americans were "scarcely capable of mental endowments." How does Banneker's letter serve to refute this belief? How would you characterize Banneker's own mental endowments?

Phillis Wheatley
On Being Brought from Africa to America   Text page 166

Sojourner Truth
Ain't I a Woman?   Text page 169

A. Understanding Main Ideas

Write the letter of the best answer to each question. (10 points each)

1. What is Wheatley's reaction to being uprooted from her native land?
   a. It was an unforeseen blessing.
   b. It made her aware of the equality of all people.
   c. It taught her that Christians are merciful and charitable.
   d. It caused her to scorn her own race.   1. _____

2. In America, Wheatley learned all of the following *except*
   a. that there is a God
   b. that there is a Savior
   c. that there is redemption
   d. that there is a sable race   2. _____

3. Wheatley's advice is directed to
   a. Christians   **c.** the sable race
   b. slaveowners   **d.** Cain   3. _____

4. Sojourner Truth believes
   a. women need to be helped into carriages and lifted over ditches
   b. men are better workers than women
   c. women are always given the best place
   d. she has worked as hard as any man   4. _____

5. What is Sojourner's main point?
   a. Women deserve the same rights as men.
   b. Women can do any job better than men can.
   c. Black women are better laborers than white women.
   d. She has as much intelligence as anyone.   5. _____

6. What is Sojourner's attitude toward intellect?
   a. Everyone has the same natural abilities.
   b. It isn't relevant to the issue of women's rights.
   c. Men are intellectually superior to women.
   d. Physical strength is more important than mental ability.   6. _____

B. Vocabulary

Each of the following sentences contains an italicized word that appears
in the selections. Choose the best synonym for each italicized word.
(10 points each)

7. Wheatley considers herself fortunate to be out of her *pagan* country.
   a. foreign   b. African   c. non-Christian   d. native   7. _____

8. Once *benighted*, Wheatley now can teach others.
   a. blind   b. ignorant   c. simple   d. unimaginative   8. _____

9. Wheatley believes that members of the *sable* race can seek salvation.
   a. primitive   c. non-Christian
   b. chosen   d. black   9. _____

10. Some people in Wheatley's day considered her skin color a *diabolic*
    characteristic.
    a. satanic   b. shameful   c. refined   d. scornful   10. _____

C. Essay

Choose one of these topics for a brief essay.

1. Unlike many other African Americans, Phillis Wheatley expresses no
   regret at leaving her native country. What words and phrases does
   Wheatley use to convey her feelings? Explain how these words
   contribute to the overall message and tone of the poem.

2. What does Sojourner Truth reveal about herself in this brief speech?
   What does she tell you about her life before she escaped to freedom?
   What impression do you get of her personality?

Frederick Douglass
from Narrative of the Life of Frederick Douglass

Text page 173

A. Understanding Main Ideas

Write the letter of the best answer to each question. (10 points each)

1. Why does Douglass stop carrying wheat to the fan?
   a. He has decided to start a revolt.
   b. There is no more wheat to feed the fan.
   c. He is completely exhausted.
   d. Another slave has taken over his job.

   1. _____

2. How does Douglass's master react to his plea for help?
   a. He sends Douglass back to Covey.
   b. He offers to protect him.
   c. He finds Douglass a new home.
   d. He gives Douglass a root to protect him from Covey.

   2. _____

3. What does Douglass consider the "turning point" in his career as a slave?
   a. Protesting Covey's abuse of him
   b. Running away from Covey
   c. Writing his autobiography
   d. Winning the fight with Covey

   3. _____

4. After the struggle in the stable, Douglass
   a. becomes a hero to the other slaves
   b. feels his spirit and confidence revived
   c. is severely punished by his own master
   d. leads a revolt against Covey

   4. _____

5. What explanation does Douglass give for not being turned over to the constable?
   a. Covey is waiting for an opportunity to be revenged.
   b. Douglass is too valuable a slave to be whipped.
   c. A public whipping would ruin Covey's reputation.
   d. Douglass is too weak to survive more punishment.

   5. _____

B. Vocabulary

Each of the following sentences contains an italicized word that appears in the selection. Choose the best synonym for each italicized word. (10 points each)

6. Douglass *intimates* that he became weak during his stay at Covey's.
   a. states outright
   c. implies
   b. declines to say
   d. protests

   6. _____

7. Douglass considers his experience at Covey's a significant *epoch* in his own history.
   a. beginning   b. moment   c. period   d. decline

   7. _____

8. Douglass's master sees that he is injured in *sundry* places.
   a. a few   b. particular   c. critical   d. various

   8. _____

9. Douglass *entreats* his owner to protect him.
   a. reasons with
   c. depends upon
   b. pleads with
   d. persuades

   9. _____

10. Douglass's sole *compensation* is satisfaction.
    a. reward   b. remembrance   c. happiness   d. pleasure

    10. _____

C. Essay

Write a brief essay on the following topic.

Douglass seeks to explain "how a slave was made a man." What do you think is Douglass's definition of "a man"? In your own words, describe the process by which Douglass achieves manhood.

African American Folk Tales

Text pages 181–185

A. Understanding Main Ideas

Write the letter of the best answer to each question. (10 points each)

1. Which of the following is particular to African American folklore?
   a. proverbs
   b. legends
   c. myths
   d. preacher tales

   1. _____

2. The hero of many African American beast fables is
   a. Brer Fox
   b. Brer Rabbit
   c. John
   d. Ole Master

   2. _____

3. Big Sixteen is named for
   a. the age at which he began working
   b. his shoe size
   c. his shirt size
   d. his height

   3. _____

4. What explanation is given for the lights you might see in the woods at night?
   a. The devil is looking for his home with a lighted torch.
   b. Big Sixteen is searching for the devil with a lantern.
   c. Big Sixteen is carrying a lit coal.
   d. They are caused by the reflection from Big Sixteen's hammer.

   4. _____

5. Why does the snake pay God a visit?
   a. He wants God to give him fangs.
   b. he wants a mate.
   c. He is not getting along with the other animals.
   d. He needs some protection.

   5. _____

6. God helps the snake by giving him
   a. poison
   b. a rattle
   c. fangs and a rattle
   d. poison and a rattle

   6. _____

7. What natural characteristic of the possum causes him to lose his bushy tail?
   a. He sleeps a lot.
   b. He is constantly underfoot.
   c. He is forgetful.
   d. He is vain about his appearance.

   7. _____

8. Noah's son uses the possum's tail
   a. to string a homemade banjo
   b. to tie sails onto the ark
   c. to make a fishing rod
   d. to create a bow for his fiddle   8. _____

9. Brer Rabbit runs over Brer 'Gator because he is fleeing from
   a. fire   **b.** hunters   **c.** trouble   **d.** Brer Fox   9. _____

10. Brer 'Gator's hide turns black after he
   a. falls in the mud
   b. gets trampled by Brer Rabbit
   c. is surrounded by smoke and fire
   d. jumps in the water to cool off   10. _____

B. Essay

Write a brief essay on this topic.

Some folk tales attribute human characteristics to nonliving things or to
animals. Choose one or more of Hurston's tales and explain the human
characteristics of the animal characters.

Spirituals

Text pages 187–190

Understanding Main Ideas

Write the letter of the best answer to each question. (10 points each)

1. The Jubilee Singers
   a. composed spirituals
   b. were a group of students
   c. helped to collect spirituals
   d. published *Slave Songs of the United States*   1. _____

2. The spirituals known as "signal" songs
   a. expressed a desire for spiritual salvation
   b. told of the oppression of the Southern slaves
   c. drew parallels between the slavery of Biblical people and Southern slaves
   d. carried messages to slaves   2. _____

3. In the spirituals, the North Star was a symbol of
   a. the Big Dipper   c. freedom
   b. redemption   d. the Underground Railroad   3. _____

4. Which of these statements is *not* accurate?
   a. Spirituals are ballads.
   b. There are no known composers of spirituals.
   c. Many spirituals exist in more than one form.
   d. Many spirituals carried a double meaning for slaves.   4. _____

5. "Go down, Moses" draws a parallel between
   a. the Israelites and the Southern slaves
   b. Moses and Pharaoh
   c. the Egyptians and the Southern slaves
   d. Egyptland and Israel   5. _____

6. In "Swing Low, Sweet Chariot," the word *home* refers to
   a. Jordan   c. heaven
   b. the speaker's native land   d. a chariot   6. _____

7. The speaker in "Steal Away" is summoned by
   a. the call of thunder
   b. a choir of angels
   c. a chariot of fire
   d. a blinding light   7. _____

8. In "I Got a Home in Dat Rock," the speaker identifies with
   a. Dives   c. the rainbow
   b. Noah   d. Lazarus   8. _____

9. The "Rainbow sign" is a reference to
   a. God's assurance that he would not send another flood
   b. Noah's Ark
   c. a second destruction by fire
   d. spiritual salvation   9. _____

10. In "I Thank God I'm Free at Las'," the speaker refers to
    a. the emancipation of slaves
    b. the judgment of sinners
    c. meeting his friends in heaven
    d. release from earthly cares   10. _____

Analogy Test 2

Recognizing Relationships in Verbal Analogies

Verbal analogies test your understanding of the relationships among words. Look at the following example:

courage : hero : : avarice : _____
a. greed   **c.** miser
b. soldier   **d.** pride

The correct answer is **c.** *Courage* is a characteristic associated with a *hero*, and *avarice* is associated with a *miser*.

The following analogy questions are based on vocabulary words taken from the selections in Unit Three. Choose the letter of the best answer to each question. (10 points each)

1. hate : detest : : implant : _____
   a. destroy   **c.** replace
   b. adore   **d.** rivet   1. _____

2. adversity : misfortune : : assailant : _____
   a. distraction   **c.** consternation
   b. attacker   **d.** delusion   2. _____

3. allay : fear : : aggravate : _____
   a. pain   **c.** nuisance
   b. hope   **d.** conviction   3. _____

4. frantic : calm : : copious : _____
   a. plenty   **c.** sparse
   b. poignant   **d.** inflexible   4. _____

5. providential : providence : : pestilential : _____
   a. pesty   **c.** pest
   b. pestilent   **d.** pestilence   5. _____

6. indispensable : essential : : solicitous : _____
   a. necessary   **c.** artificial
   b. concerned   **d.** vague   6. _____

7. benighted : ignorant : : poignant : _____
   a. evil   **c.** graceful
   b. painful   **d.** illiterate   7. _____

8. commodious : cramped :: diabolic : _____
   a. satanic   c. angelic
   b. sable   d. pagan   8. _____

9. interpose : dispose :: respiration : _____
   a. perspiration   c. breathing
   b. intersperse   d. render   9. _____

10. curry : horse :: flog : _____
    a. whip   c. groom
    b. constable   d. servant   10. _____

RECONSTRUCTION TO RENAISSANCE
Introduction

Understanding Main Ideas

Write the letter of the best answer to each question. (10 points each)

1. After the Civil War, Southerners
   a. were denied citizenship in the nation
   b. accepted the North's plan of Reconstruction
   c. chose their own brand of Reconstruction
   d. accepted black Americans as citizens   1. _____

2. "Black codes" were meant
   a. to demonstrate equality of blacks and whites
   b. to reassert white control over black Americans
   c. to show sympathy toward black Americans
   d. to restore slavery   2. _____

3. The Freedmen's Bureau was established to do all of the following *except*
   a. create schools for black Americans
   b. help black Americans buy land
   c. supervise contracts for black Americans
   d. give black Americans the right to vote   3. _____

4. Black Americans who went to urban areas to find work after the Civil
   War found
   a. competition with white workers
   b. good job opportunities
   c. the same work as in rural areas
   d. many managerial positions   4. _____

5. Eventually the Southern economy was strengthened by
   a. sharecroppers   **c.** the cotton industry
   b. new black farm owners   **d.** new civil rights bills   5. _____

6. A strong believer that black Americans could improve their situation by
   working within the existing system was
   a. Frederick Douglass   **c.** W. E. B. Du Bois
   b. Rutherford B. Hayes   **d.** Booker T. Washington   6. _____

7. The National Association for the Advancement of Colored People was founded by
   a. Booker T. Washington
   b. Charles Sumner
   c. W. E. B. Du Bois
   d. Martin Luther King, Jr.

   7. _____

8. In reaction to stereotyping by whites, black fiction writers relied on
   a. idealization
   b. "down home" poetry
   c. negative propaganda
   d. drama

   8. _____

9. The most famous black American poet of the era was
   a. Booker T. Washington
   b. Charles W. Chesnutt
   c. Ida B. Wells
   d. Paul Laurence Dunbar

   9. _____

10. During his own age, Dunbar was best known for
    a. writing in standard English
    b. novels and essays
    c. poems in picturesque dialect
    d. protest poetry

    10. _____

Booker T. Washington
from **Up from Slavery**

Text page 214

A. Understanding Main Ideas

Write the letter of the best answer to each question. (10 points each)

1. Freed slaves found it necessary to leave the plantation because
   a. they wished to go to the North
   b. they needed to prove that they were really free
   c. plantation owners forced them to leave
   d. there was no more work available   1. _____

2. Washington's family found that living conditions outside the plantation were
   a. always better   c. usually improved
   b. sanitary and clean   d. often even worse   2. _____

3. As a child, the one thing Washington wanted more than anything else was
   a. new clothes   c. interesting work
   b. to learn to read   d. to write a book   3. _____

4. Washington got most of his education by
   a. going to night school
   b. going to Sunday school
   c. teaching himself
   d. attending day school with the other children   4. _____

5. Young Booker helped support his family by
   a. teaching school
   b. working in a mine
   c. making clothes
   d. reading for the townspeople   5. _____

B. Vocabulary

Each of the following sentences contains an italicized word that appears in the selection. Choose the best synonym for each italicized word. (10 points each)

6. Until he attended school, Washington did not have a *surname*.
   a. middle name
   b. family name
   c. first name
   d. nickname

   6. _____

7. After leaving the plantations, many families made *tedious* journeys to find new homes.
   a. long   b. difficult   c. tiresome   d. dangerous

   7. _____

8. Washington's mother was able to *procure* a spelling book for him.
   a. obtain   b. buy   c. borrow   d. copy

   8. _____

9. Washington believed that he inherited his *disposition* from his mother.
   a. ambition
   b. creativity
   c. temperament
   d. appearance

   9. _____

10. The desire to read the Bible served as an important *stimulus* for people of the older generation.
    a. obstacle   b. reason   c pattern   d. incentive

    10. _____

C. Essay

Choose of these topics for a brief essay.

1. In Booker T. Washington's time, newly freed slaves faced many hardships. Which of these difficulties does Washington focus on in the chapter from his autobiography? Which do you think were the greatest problems faced by the freedmen?

2. Washington believed that ex-slaves could help themselves to get ahead. Which characteristics did he approve of? Refer to specific evidence in the selection to support your statements.

Charles W. Chesnutt
The Bouquet

Text page 228

A. Understanding Main Ideas

Write the letter of the best answer to each question. (10 points each)

1. The Myrovers lost most of their money because
   a. their plantation was burned during the Civil War
   b. women could not inherit money
   c. Colonel Myrover had invested in Confederate bonds
   d. Mrs. Myrover made bad investments

   1. _____

2. Miss Mary decides to teach black children despite
   a. the disapproval of her mother
   b. the low salary
   c. the fact that she is ill
   d. the unwillingness of the children to learn

   2. _____

3. Sophy's attitude toward Miss Mary might best be described as
   a. curious   b. civil   c. hostile   d. devoted

   3. _____

4. Mary's mother blames her daughter's death on
   a. Mary's illness
   b. Mary's work as a teacher
   c. an accident
   d. herself

   4. _____

5. Sophy is not allowed to attend the funeral because
   a. blacks are never allowed in the church
   b. it is too crowded
   c. Mrs. Myrover refuses to let children attend
   d. Mrs. Myrover refuses to let any blacks attend

   5. _____

B. Vocabulary

Each of the following sentences contains an italicized word that appears in the selection. Choose the best synonym for each italicized word. (10 points each)

6. Mrs. Myrover never *concedes* the right of blacks to attend school.
   a. opposes   **b.** understands   **c.** acknowledges   **d.** denies

   6. _____

7. Mary Myrover is *fortified* by her experiences during her first day as a teacher.
   a. strengthened   **c.** puzzled
   b. threatened   **d.** angered

   7. _____

8. Sophy's feelings for her teacher are *manifested* in many different ways.
   a. dramatized   **c.** shown
   b. disguised   **d.** ridiculed

   8. _____

9. Prince enjoys chasing rabbits, *presumably* for exercise.
   a. intentionally   **c.** probably
   b. frequently   **d.** actually

   9. _____

10. Sophy makes a *conscientious* effort to please her teacher.
   a. futile   **c.** partial
   b. careful   **d.** renewed

   10. _____

C. Essay

Write a brief essay on this topic.

"The Bouquet" tells of the relationship between a black child and her white teacher. How would you describe their relationship? If Miss Myrover had lived longer, do you think the two would have become closer? Why or why not?

Ida B. Wells
from Crusade for Justice

Text page 240

A. Understanding Main Ideas

Write the letter of the best answer to each question. (10 points each)

1. By taking a seat in the ladies' coach, Wells
   a. was deliberately breaking the law
   b. wished to draw attention to segregated railroad cars
   c. knew that she would be asked to leave
   d. was acting as usual

   1. _____

2. When Wells refused to move, the conductor
   a. let her stay in her seat
   b. asked her to leave the train
   c. attempted to force her out of her seat
   d. told her to go to the back of the car

   2. _____

3. Wells's first lawyer did not pursue her case because
   a. he did not believe her story
   b. he was bought off by the railroad
   c. she found another lawyer
   d. he knew that it was impossible to win the case

   3. _____

4. Although Wells won her case in the circuit court,
   a. the railroad appealed the case and won
   b. the railroad refused to pay damages
   c. the case went to the United States Supreme Court, where she lost
   d. she dropped charges against the railroad

   4. _____

5. The railroad fought Wells's case by every means possible to avoid
   a. losing great sums of money in damages
   b. more negative publicity
   c. establishing a custom for others to follow
   d. repeal of the Civil Rights Bill

   5. _____

B. Vocabulary

Each of the following sentences contains an italicized word that appears in the selection. Choose the best definition for each italicized word. (10 points each)

6. Wells refused to *compromise* by taking money from the railroad.
   a. let an opponent win
   b. give up a fight knowingly
   c. make concessions
   d. participate in an illegal action   6. _____

7. Wells was the *plaintiff* in an historic case.
   a. accused in a civil trial
   b. party who brings suit against another
   c. winner in a court case
   d. loser in a court case   7. _____

8. The Chesapeake and Ohio Railroad feared that Wells's case would set a *precedent*.
   a. lengthy struggle
   b. decision carrying heavy fines
   c. threat to civil rights
   d. legal decision that establishes a custom   8. _____

9. Wells sought *redress* by suing the railroad.
   a. satisfaction for wrongs done
   b. heavy damages
   c. public recognition
   d. new standing   9. _____

10. In the end, Wells realized that black Americans had few ways to deal with their *grievances*.
    a. problems   c. complaints
    b. legal wrongs   d. needs   10. _____

C. Essay

Write an essay on the following topic.

What can you tell about Wells's character from this episode? Give a brief description of Wells, focusing on the characteristics she displays in her narrative. Refer to specific evidence in the autobiography to support your statements.

W. E. B. Du Bois
The Song of the Smoke

Text page 245

An Open-Book Test

A. Understanding Poetic Technique

Write the letter of the best answer to each question. (10 points each)

1. In lines 3–4, Du Bois uses all of the following poetic devices *except*
   a. rhyme   **c.** repetition
   b. alliteration   **d.** simile   1. _____

2. The refrain of the poem first appears in
   a. lines 1–2   **c.** lines 10–11
   b. lines 5–6   **d.** lines 41–42   2. _____

3. An example of alliteration appears in
   a. line 11   **c.** line 20
   b. line 14   **d.** line 24   3. _____

4. Personification is used in all of the following lines *except*
   a. line 1   **c.** line 13
   b. line 5   **d.** line 28   4. _____

5. The rhyme pattern in lines 3–4 is repeated in each of the following
   except
   a. lines 5–6   **c.** lines 25–26
   b. lines 14–15   **d.** lines 36–37   5. _____

B. Vocabulary

Match the words in the left column with their synonyms in the right column. Write the letter of the correct answer in the space provided. (10 points each)

6. sheathe	a. listen	6. _____
7. sod	b. dirt-covered	7. _____
8. hearken	c. reddish	8. _____
9. ruddy	d. shroud	9. _____
10. grimy	e. enclose	10. _____
	f. grass-covered soil	
	g. smearing	

Paul Laurence Dunbar

An Open-Book Test

A. Understanding Main Ideas

Write the letter of the best answer to each question. (10 points each)

1. In "We Wear the Mask," the mask refers to
   a. true feelings
   b. a copy of a face
   c. the hidden self
   d. the smile that the outer world is shown

   1. _____

2. The mask conceals
   a. feelings of pain
   b. years of regret
   c. unfulfilled dreams
   d. feelings of sympathy

   2. _____

3. Which lines in "The Debt" identify what is owed?
   a. Lines 1–2   c. Lines 7–8
   b. Lines 3–4   d. Lines 11–12

   3. _____

4. The phrase "deeper griefs" in line 4 of "Life's Tragedy" refers to
   a. never being loved
   b. never singing
   c. missing perfect love and song
   d. missing youth

   4. _____

5. The narrator of "Douglass" compares the famous orator to
   a. a storm-tossed ship
   b. a ship's pilot
   c. the stars
   d. the wind

   5. _____

B. Vocabulary

Each of the following sentences contains an italicized word that appears in the poems. Choose the best synonym for each italicized word. (10 points each)

6. "We Wear the Mask" describes a type of *guile*.
   a. crime   **b.** revenge   **c.** anger   **d.** deceit

   6. _____

7. In "The Debt," one *riotous* occasion is paid for dearly.
   a. funny   **b.** uproarious   **c.** crowded   **d.** murderous

   7. _____

8. The loss of perfection results in "*potent* sorrow."
   a. powerful   **c.** unspoken
   b. everlasting   **d.** tragic

   8. _____

9. The poem "Douglass" compares a time of *dispraise* to a storm.
   a. loss   **b.** war   **c.** revolution   **d.** reproach

   9. _____

10. The narrator of "Douglass" fears the *dissension* of the times.
    a. destruction   **c.** conflict
    b. rumors   **d.** lack of communication

    10. _____

John Henry

Text page 259

A. Understanding Main Ideas

Write the letter of the best answer to each question. (10 points each)

1. The story of John Henry is told chiefly by
   a. his wife
   b. the foreman
   c. John Henry himself
   d. an unidentified narrator

   1. _____

2. Which of the following is *not* a characteristic of folk ballads?
   a. The story is often sad.
   b. The story is told through dialogue and action.
   c. The poem has abrupt transitions.
   d. The language is sophisticated.

   2. _____

3. Why does John Henry become a legend?
   a. He destroys a mountain with his hammer.
   b. He outwits the captain.
   c. He challenges a steam drill.
   d. He races a locomotive.

   3. _____

4. According to the rock at Big Ben Tunnel, John Henry was from
   a. Alabama   c. East Virginia
   b. Georgia   d. the East

   4. _____

5. When he first starts working, John Henry is discouraged because
   a. the mountain is huge
   b. he needs a pick and shovel
   c. the work is too difficult
   d. the rock is too hard

   5. _____

6. How does John Henry die?
   a. He is trapped by a cave-in.
   b. He drops dead from exhaustion.
   c. He is injured by the steam drill.
   d. He loses his footing and falls off the mountain.

   6. _____

7. Which of the following statements does *not* describe John Henry's wife?
   a. She has small feet.
   b. She has rosy cheeks.
   c. She is dressed in blue.
   d. She wears a large straw hat.

   7. _____

8. The last thing John Henry's wife tells him is
   a. her father will buy her shoes
   b. her mother will give her gloves
   c. her sister will kiss her
   d. she will never love another man

   8. _____

9. When they hear of John Henry's death, women in the West
   a. stop trains going east
   b. dress in black
   c. boycott the railroad
   d. hold a big funeral for him

   9. _____

10. John Henry's body is taken
    a. back to the mountain   c. to the White House
    b. to his family   d. to the West

    10. _____

B. Essay

Write a brief essay on this topic. You may refer to the poem as often as you wish.

Many legends are based on the lives of real people. Over generations of storytelling, fiction becomes mixed with fact. How much of the John Henry story do you think is true, and how much do you think is invented? Tell what you think actually happened. Refer to specific lines in the poem.

Analogy Test 3

Recognizing Relationships in Verbal Analogies

Choose the letter of the best answer to each question. (10 points each)

1. indulge : desire :: confront : _____
   a. opponent   **b.** face   **c.** disposition   **d.** grace

   1. _____

2. intrinsic : essential :: profuse : _____
   a. important   **b.** scanty   **c.** abundant   **d.** fundamental

   2. _____

3. fortify : strengthen :: contravene : _____
   a. dare   **b.** travel   **c.** dress   **d.** oppose

   3. _____

4. rector : parish :: sexton : _____
   a. church property   **c.** janitor
   b. official   **d.** church services

   4. _____

5. redress : grievance :: solve : _____
   a. precedent   **b.** plaintiff   **c.** problem   **d.** case

   5. _____

6. compromise : settle :: concede : _____
   a. acknowledge   **b.** refuse   **c.** argue   **d.** assume

   6. _____

7. hearken : ignore :: sheathe : _____
   a. stab   **b.** protect   **c.** uncover   **d.** divide

   7. _____

8. ruddy : grimy :: motley : _____
   a. livery   **b.** tedious   **c.** subtlety   **d.** indignantly

   8. _____

9. guile : truth :: potent : _____
   a. vile   **b.** plenty   **c.** powerful   **d.** weak

   9. _____

10. dissension : harmony :: dispraise : _____
    a. approval   **b.** noise   **c.** stimulus   **d** honesty

    10. _____

THE HARLEM RENAISSANCE
Introduction

Understanding Main Ideas

Write the letter of the best answer to each question. (10 points each)

1. The Great Migration refers to
   a. the flow of European immigrants to the United States
   b. the push westward of pioneers
   c. a movement of black Americans from the South to the North
   d. the arrival of intellectuals in Harlem   1. _____

2. Alain Locke
   a. gave the name Harlem Renaissance to the period
   b. edited an important anthology of black writers
   c. founded *The Crisis*
   d. organized Pan African conferences   2. _____

3. Harlem became known as all of the following *except*
   a. the Chicago of the East
   b. the Mecca of the New Negro
   c. the City of Refuge
   d. the Promised Land   3. _____

4. The most important musical development of the period was
   a. gospel   b. spirituals   c. jazz   d. Dixieland   4. _____

5. Women writers of the period included all of the following *except*
   a. Jessie Fauset   c. Zora Neale Hurston
   b. Nella Larsen   d. Harriet A. Jacobs   5. _____

6. Marcus Garvey founded
   a. the National Association for the Advancement of Colored People
   b. the Universal Negro Improvement Association
   c. the National Urban League
   d. the National Association of Colored Women's Clubs   6. _____

7. An African American poet who tended to use the sonnet form was
   a. James Weldon Johnson   c. Jean Toomer
   b. Langston Hughes   d. Claude McKay   7. _____

8. Writers who adapted traditional oral forms in their writing included all of the following *except*
   a. James Weldon Johnson
   b. Sterling A. Brown
   c. Zora Neale Hurston
   d. Claude McKay

   8. _____

9. The writer who defined the dilemma of black American identity was
   a. W. E. B. Du Bois
   b. Countee Cullen
   c. Nella Larsen
   d. Jessie Fauset

   9. _____

10. Which of the following pairs is correct?
    a. Langston Hughes: *Cane*
    b. Zora Neale Hurston: *Mules and Men*
    c. Rudolph Fisher: *Home to Harlem*
    d. Jean Toomer: *The Souls of Black Folk*

    10. _____

NAME _____ CLASS _____ DATE _____

SCORE _____

James Weldon Johnson
Text pages 281–293

An Open-Book Test

A. Understanding Ideas and Poetic Techniques

Write the letter of the best answer to each question. (5 points each)

1. The bards in "O Black and Unknown Bards" are
   a. anonymous composers of spirituals
   b. minstrel poets of the Middle Ages
   c. ancient epic poets
   d. Johnson's contemporaries   1. _____

2. "O Black and Unknown Bards" refers to all of the following spirituals
   except
   a. "Swing Low, Sweet Chariot"
   b. "Steal Away"
   c. "Go Down, Moses"
   d. "I Thank God I'm Free at Las'"   2. _____

3. Which of the following statements is *not* an accurate description of "O
   Black and Unknown Bards"?
   a. All stanzas have the same number of lines.
   b. The rhyme pattern is the same in each stanza.
   c. The first two lines in each stanza rhyme.
   d. Each of the first three stanzas contains a series of questions.   3. _____

4. In "O Black and Unknown Bards," inversion is illustrated in
   a. line 33   c. line 41
   b. line 36   d. line 47   4. _____

5. In "The Creation," lines 7–8 illustrate all of the following poetic devices
   except
   a. exaggeration   c. alliteration
   b. personification   d. simile   5. _____

6. The line that functions as a refrain in "The Creation" is
   a. line 13   c. line 53
   b. line 48   d. line 69   6. _____

7. According to Johnson's poem, God created human beings
   a. in a garden   c. in a cypress swamp
   b. beside a river   d. on the side of a hill   7. _____

8. Which of the following statements is an accurate description of "Lift Every Voice and Sing"?
   a. All stanzas have the same number of lines.
   b. The last two lines in each stanza rhyme.
   c. The third and sixth lines in each stanza rhyme.
   d. The poem is written in free verse.   8. _____

9. Which of the following lines in "Lift Every Voice and Sing" illustrates alliteration?
   a. Line 1   c. Line 6
   b. Line 3   d. Line 10   9. _____

10. Parallelism is illustrated in all of the following *except*
   a. lines 7–8   c. lines 19–20
   b. lines 17–18   d. lines 32–33   10. _____

B. Vocabulary

Match the words in the left column with their definitions in the right column. (10 points each)

11. elusive   a. lacking vegetation   11. _____

12. servile   b. punishing   12. _____

13. barren   c. rhythmic shouting   13. _____

14. chant   d. submissive   14. _____

15. chastening   e. sparkling   15. _____

                          f. difficult to describe

                          g. lump of earth

C. Essay

Write a brief essay on this topic.

The three poems in your anthology give you some idea of Johnson's range and diversity. Discuss Johnson's different poetic styles. Refer to such elements as diction, stanzaic forms, rhyme schemes, and inversion.

Claude McKay

Text pages 298–300

An Open-Book Test

A. Understanding Ideas and Poetic Techniques

Write the letter of the best answer to each question. (10 points each)

1. What is the speaker looking at in "The Tropics in New York"?
   a. Photographs of fruit trees
   b. Travel posters
   c. Displays of fruit in a store window
   d. A street cart filled with tropical fruits

   1. _____

2. Which of the following statements is *not* an accurate description of "The Tropics in New York"?
   a. The poem consists of three stanzas.
   b. The rhyme scheme is the same in each stanza.
   c. The poem contains a refrain.
   d. The imagery of the poem is chiefly visual.

   2. _____

3. The "Red aspish tongues" in line 10 of "Baptism" are
   a. a reference to smoke
   b. a metaphor for flames
   c. the speaker's enemies
   d. a symbol of poisonous gossip

   3. _____

4. In "If We Must Die," the "murderous, cowardly pack" most likely refers to
   a. wild animals   c. hired assassins
   b. an enemy army   d. a lynch mob

   4. _____

5. The enemy is referred to in all of the following lines *except*
   a. line 3   c. line 9
   b. line 5   d. line 13

   5. _____

6. In "America," each of these lines illustrates personification *except*
   a. line 1   c. line 8
   b. line 6   d. line 13

   6. _____

7. Which of the following pairs is accurate?
   a. "The Tropics in New York": lyric
   b. "Baptism": Shakespearean sonnet
   c. "If We Must Die": Petrarchan sonnet
   d. "America": Petrarchan sonnet

7. _____

B. Vocabulary

Match the words in the left column with their definitions in the right column. (6 points each)

8. rill   a. trick   8. _____

9. benediction   b. wonderful   9. _____

10. inglorious   c. not honorable   10. _____

11. unerring   d. blessing   11. _____

12. jeer   e. small brook   12. _____

                           f. exact

                           g. derisive comment

C. Essay

A paraphrase is a summary or restatement of a piece of work. When you paraphrase, you restate the author's language and ideas in your own words. Write a paraphrase of one of McKay's poems. Restate all images and figures of speech in plain language.

Jean Toomer

Text pages 305–309

An Open-Book Test

A. Understanding Ideas and Poetic Techniques

Write the letter of the best answer to each question. (10 points each)

1. Line 8 of "Beehive" illustrates
   a. metaphor only
   b. alliteration only
   c. both alliteration and figurative language
   d. assonance chiefly   1. _____

2. In "Beehive," an image that appeals to the sense of hearing occurs in
   a. line 3   c. line 11
   b. line 6   d. line 13   2. _____

3. In "Beehive," the poet uses alliteration in each of the following lines
   except
   a. line 1   c. line 7
   b. line 6   d. line 14   3. _____

4. How many different rhymes are found in "November Cotton Flower"?
   a. Four   b. Five   c. Six   d. Seven   4. _____

5. In "November Cotton Flower," the subject of the verb *was vanishing* in
   line 4 is
   a. southern snow, line 3
   b. winter's cold, line 1
   c. cotton, line 3
   d. the branch, line 4   5. _____

6. The blooming of the flower is unusual because
   a. there has been a dry period
   b. dead birds have been found in wells
   c. no cotton was planted
   d. the boll weevil has destroyed all the plants   6. _____

7. In "Reapers," the word *Blood-stained* in line 8 refers to
   a. weeds, line 10
   b. field rat, line 6
   c. blade, line 7
   d. belly, line 7   7. _____

8. Lines 1–2 of "Reapers" illustrate all of the following techniques *except*

    a. end rhyme   **c.** alliteration

    b. internal rhyme   **d.** assonance   **8.** _____

9. Which of the following statements about "Song of the Son" is accurate?

    a. All stanzas contain the same number of lines.

    b. The rhyme scheme is consistent throughout the poem.

    c. The second and third lines of each stanza rhyme.

    d. The poet does not repeat any rhymes.   **9.** _____

10. Lines 19–20 in "Song of the Son" illustrate all of the following techniques *except*

    a. alliteration   **c.** metaphor

    b. assonance   **d.** simile   **10.** _____

B. Essay

Write a brief essay on the following topic.

Rhyme and other devices of repetition can create pleasure and can also enhance a poem's meaning. Consider the effects of sound in Toomer's poetry. How does he use devices of sound to convey a particular mood or to excite emotions in the reader? Refer to specific evidence in the poems.

Langston Hughes
When the Negro Was in Vogue

Text page 314

A. Understanding Main Ideas

Write the letter of the best answer to each question. (10 points each)

1. According to Hughes, the Harlem Renaissance was launched by
   a. jazz musicians
   b. a play by the Provincetown Players
   c. a dance
   d. a musical revue

   1. _____

2. What did Bessie Smith and Clara Smith have in common?
   a. They were stars of musical comedy.
   b. They were blues singers.
   c. They were noted actresses.
   d. They were mother and daughter.

   2. _____

3. Hughes did not go to the Cotton Club because
   a. it was a segregated nightclub
   b. it was too expensive
   c. it was crowded with too many tourists
   d. the performers were too commercial

   3. _____

4. According to Hughes, the clubs in Harlem
   a. lost business when they excluded blacks
   b. were owned by gangsters and monied whites
   c. never admitted black customers
   d. were patronized mainly by celebrities

   4. _____

5. Hughes believes that in the attempt to entertain whites, black performers
   a. became stars
   b. lost their integrity
   c. developed as artists
   d. failed to impress their white audiences

   5. _____

6. Which of the following statements is *not* one of Hughes's conclusions?
   a. Most blacks were unaffected by the vogue.
   b. Harlem was a victim of its own vogue.
   c. The race problem was solved through art.
   d. Most black Harlemites resented the influx of white tourists.

   6. _____

B. Vocabulary

Each of the following sentences contains an italicized word that appears in the selection. Choose the best definition or description for each italicized word. (8 points each)

7. A *prima donna* is usually found
   a. in a circus
   b. in a cabaret
   c. in a nightclub
   d. in an opera house

   7. _____

8. Black customers found that some club owners in Harlem were not *cordial*.
   a. polite   c. well known
   b. satisfied   d. pleased

   8. _____

9. Hughes believed that the *vogue* would not last.
   a. entertainment   c. fashion
   b. mood   d. interest

   9. _____

10. According to Hughes, many writers *distorted* their material.
    a. rewrote   c. over-colored
    b. misrepresented   d. destroyed

    10. _____

11. Hughes thought that one of the revues was a *scintillating* show.
    a. sparkling   c. remarkable
    b. popular   d. great

    11. _____

C. Essay

Write a brief essay on this topic.

A writer's attitude toward a subject or toward the reader is shown through the selection of details and through the choice of words with certain emotional associations. Discuss Hughes's tone in this excerpt from *The Big Sea*. Refer to specific evidence in the selection. Also tell if you think his tone is effective.

Langston Hughes
Five Poems

Text pages 322–327

An Open-Book Test

Understanding Ideas and Poetic Techniques

Write the letter of the best answer to each question. (10 points each)

1. The rivers mentioned in "The Negro Speaks of Rivers" are located in all
   of the following lands *except*
   a. Africa   **c.** South America
   b. Asia   **d.** North America   1. _____

2. The phrase "muddy bosom" in "The Negro Speaks of Rivers" is an
   example of
   a. alliteration   **c.** simile
   b. repetition   **d.** personification   2. _____

3. In "Harlem," Hughes uses alliteration in all of the following lines *except*
   a. line 1   **c.** line 5
   b. line 2   **d.** line 8   3. _____

4. The poetic device that appears with greatest frequency in "Harlem" is
   a. simile   **c.** rhyme
   b. assonance   **d.** metaphor   4. _____

5. Which of the following statements about "Dreams" is *not* accurate?
   a. Many of the words have unpleasant connotations.
   b. The poet uses end rhyme.
   c. Both stanzas have parallel structure.
   d. Each stanza contains a metaphor.   5. _____

6. The central idea of "I, Too" is that of
   a. a dream that has been destroyed
   b. a family that treats its members unfairly
   c. the tyranny of slavery
   d. the fulfillment of the American dream   6. _____

7. Which of the following is the best interpretation for lines 9–10 in
   "I, Too"?
   a. The speaker will finally get enough food to eat.
   b. The speaker will become a welcome guest.
   c. The company will eat in the kitchen.
   d. One day there will be equal rights for all Americans.   7. _____

8. For the speaker of "I, Too," eating in the kitchen represents
   a. getting scraps
   b. humiliation
   c. growing strong
   d. a loss of identity   8. _____

9. In "Mother to Son," the phrase "crystal stair"
   a. is a metaphor for the good life
   b. represents the fragility of hope
   c. stands for the speaker's goal
   d. is a symbol of the speaker's life   9. _____

10. The word *Bare* in line 7 refers to
    a. *carpet,* line 6
    b. *boards,* line 5
    c. *places,* line 6
    d. *Life,* line 2   10. _____

Countee Cullen

Text pages 337–342

An Open-Book Test

A. Understanding Ideas and Poetic Techniques

Write the letter of the best answer to each question. (10 points each)

1. In "From the Dark Tower," the phrase "abject and mute" refers to
   a. *fruit,* line 2
   b. *We,* line 1
   c. *countenance,* line 3
   d. *plant,* line 1

   1. _____

2. The rhyme scheme of "From the Dark Tower" is
   a. abba cddc eeffgg
   b. abba cddc effegg
   c. abab abab cdecde
   d. abba abba ccddee

   2. _____

3. In "Yet Do I Marvel," the phrase "flesh that mirrors Him" in line 4 refers to
   a. Tantalus   c. human beings
   b. Sisyphus   d. the mole

   3. _____

4. The "curious thing" in "Yet Do I Marvel" is
   a. poetic inspiration
   b. the suffering of helpless creatures
   c. the whims of fate
   d. life's ironies

   4. _____

5. Which of the following statements about "Incident" is *not* accurate?
   a. The speaker stayed in Baltimore for eight months.
   b. The speaker tried to befriend another child.
   c. The speaker has many fond memories of his trip.
   d. The speaker was permanently affected by an offensive experience.

   5. _____

6. Which of these statements is correct?
   a. "From the Dark Tower" and "Yet Do I Marvel" are Petrarchan sonnets.
   b. "From the Dark Tower" and "Yet Do I Marvel" are Shakespearean sonnets.
   c. "From the Dark Tower" is a Shakespearean sonnet; "Yet Do I Marvel" is a Petrarchan sonnet.
   d. "From the Dark Tower" is a Petrarchan sonnet; "Yet Do I Marvel" is a Shakespearean sonnet.

   6. _____

B. Vocabulary

Choose the phrase that gives the best definition or explanation of the italicized word. (10 points each)

7. To become *abject* is to become
   a. dejected and wretched
   b. confused
   c. indignant
   d. self-conscious

   7. _____

8. To *quibble* is
   a. to question the meaning of something
   b. to argue over small details
   c. to establish or set rules
   d. to answer all questions

   8. _____

9. A *fickle* admirer is
   a. devoted
   b. changeable
   c. sensible
   d. unrealistic

   9. _____

10. *Petty* concerns are
    a. urgent   b. awful   c. compelling   d. trivial

    10. _____

C. Essay

Choose one of Cullen's poem and write a paraphrase, restating its language and ideas in your own words.

Zora Neale Hurston
from Dust Tracks on a Road

Text page 347

A. Understanding Main Ideas

Write the letter of the best answer to each question. (10 points each)

1. Zora Neale Hurston's grandmother worried about her because
   a. she never asked permission to leave the house
   b. she was constantly getting into mischief
   c. she was a lazy student
   d. she would ask white travelers if she could accompany them

   1. _____

2. When visitors came to the school, the students always
   a. read from their readers
   b. sang a spiritual
   c. recited poems
   d. answered questions politely

   2. _____

3. Which of the following statements is *not* true?
   a. Zora disliked writing.
   b. She enjoyed geography.
   c. She liked dressing up.
   d. A favorite part of her school day was recess.

   3. _____

4. During her visit to the Park House, Zora was asked to do all of the following *except*
   a. write a thank-you note
   b. read from a magazine
   c. have her picture taken
   d. eat special delicacies

   4. _____

5. Of the books she received as gifts, Zora most enjoyed
   a. a book of hymns
   b. moral tales about sweet and gentle girls
   c. myths, fairy tales, and stories of fantasy
   d. historical stories set in the distant past

   5. _____

B. Vocabulary

Each of the following sentences contains an italicized word or phrase that appears in the selection. Choose the best synonym for each italicized word or phrase. (10 points each)

6. Zora's grandmother considered her behavior *brazen*.
   a. silly   **b.** impudent   **c.** frightening   **d.** unfeminine   6. _____

7. Mr. Calhoun became *flustered* when visitors arrived unexpectedly.
   a. annoyed   **b.** speechless   **c.** angry   **d.** confused   7. _____

8. Zora was stirred *profoundly* by the story of Hercules.
   a. deeply   **b.** unexpectedly   **c.** sincerely   **d.** chiefly   8. _____

9. Zora *resolved* to imitate one of her favorite characters.
   a. liked   **b.** wanted   **c.** agreed   **d.** decided   9. _____

10. Zora could not *conceive of* death.
    a. think about   **c.** imagine
    b. understand   **d.** forget about   10. _____

C. Essay

Write a brief essay on this topic.

At the opening of the selection, Zora Neale Hurston says that she liked to sit on the gate-post and "watch the world go by." How does she show that as a youngster she had a lively mind and an interest in the world outside her village?

Rudolph Fisher
Miss Cynthie

Text page 357

A. Understanding Main Ideas

Write the letter of the best answer to each question. (10 points each)

1. At the opening of the story, Miss Cynthie
   a. has been traveling for two days
   b. insists on carrying her own bags
   c. walks with a cane
   d. is looking for a taxi

   1. _____

2. Miss Cynthie hopes her grandson
   a. is studying to become a preacher
   b. is an undertaker
   c. is a tooth-doctor
   d. is in show business

   2. _____

3. What Miss Cynthie enjoys most about the ride uptown is
   a. the tall buildings
   b. Central Park
   c. the traffic lights
   d. the speed of Dave's car

   3. _____

4. Dave Tappen lives
   a. in a mansion on Central Park West
   b. in a tall apartment building overlooking a park
   c. next to St. Mark's Church
   d. on the street where the Harlem theaters are located

   4. _____

5. The audience in the Lafayette Theatre
   a. is segregated
   b. is chiefly black
   c. is enthusiastic
   d. is noisy and rude

   5. _____

6. Miss Cynthie learns
   a. that Dave and Ruth are secretly married
   b. that Dave is a comic
   c. that Dave is a movie star
   d. that Dave is a well-known musical comedy star

   6. _____

7. At the end of the story, Miss Cynthie
    a. accepts a leaf from a flower
    b. joins Dave on the stage to sing a song
    c. decides to return home to the South
    d. teaches the audience a rhyme   **7.** _____

B. Vocabulary

Each of the following sentences contains an italicized word that appears in the selection. Choose the best synonym for each italicized word. (6 points each)

8. The walk toward the exit-gate seemed *interminable*.
    a. unexpectedly short   **c.** extremely difficult
    b. without end   **d.** unusually complicated   **8.** _____

9. Miss Cynthie's voice was softened by *apprehension*.
    a. warm affection   **c.** an anxious feeling
    b. expectation   **d.** calmness   **9.** _____

10. The buildings along Seventh Avenue looked *supercilious*.
    a. towering   **c.** different
    b. miraculous   **d.** haughty   **10.** _____

11. The automobiles were *tumultuous*.
    a. noisy   **c.** colorful
    b. speeding   **d.** impatient   **11.** _____

12. Miss Cynthie sang a *jaunty* tune.
    a. lovely   **c.** familiar
    b. perky   **d.** favorite   **12.** _____

Analogy Test 4

Recognizing Relationships in Verbal Analogies

Write the letter of the best answer to each question. (10 points each)

1. exotic : lands :: elusive : _____
   a. illusive   **c.** spectacles
   b. spontaneity   **d.** pleasures   1. _____

2. pervasive : invasive :: recessional : _____
   a. imposing   **c.** church hymn
   b. processional   **d.** involuntary   2. _____

3. voluminous : correspondence :: redoubtable : _____
   a. opponent   **c.** letter
   b. respectful   **d.** countenance   3. _____

4. sallow : sickly :: spry : _____
   a. active   **b.** tedious   **c.** impious   **d.** pallid   4. _____

5. resolute : resolutely :: incredulous : _____
   a. incredible   **c.** incredulously
   b. credibility   **d.** unbelievable   5. _____

6. indifferent : significant :: degraded : _____
   a. important   **c.** trivial
   b. noble   **d.** servile   6. _____

7. barren : fertile :: desolate : _____
   a. abundant   **c.** land
   b. sterile   **d.** emptiness   7. _____

8. incoherency : clarity :: benediction : _____
   a. disorder   **b.** parish   **c.** vow   **d.** curse   8. _____

9. inglorious : glorious :: indifferent : _____
   a. different   **c.** concerned
   b. differing   **d.** distant   9. _____

10. monarch : ruler :: realm : _____
    a. leader   **c.** kinsman
    b. kingdom   **d.** ministry   10. _____

FROM RENAISSANCE TO MID-FORTIES
Introduction

Unit Six

Understanding Main Ideas

Write the letter of the best answer to each question. (10 points each)

1. Blacks who fled the South were trying to escape from all of the following *except*
   a. boll weevils
   b. sharecropping
   c. overcrowded tenements
   d. the Ku Klux Klan

   1. _____

2. The "compromise" of 1876 resulted in
   a. the granting of equal rights to black citizens
   b. the election of Rutherford B. Hayes to the presidency
   c. employment opportunities for black Americans
   d. the desegregation of public schools

   2. _____

3. Which of the following pairs is *not* correct?
   a. Franklin Delano Roosevelt: New Deal
   b. Gunnar Myrdal: *What the Negro Wants*
   c. Mary McLeod Bethune: Black Cabinet
   d. Alain Locke: *The New Negro*

   3. _____

4. In the 1930s, some black Americans were attracted to the Communist Party because
   a. they approved of atheism
   b. they supported Soviet political policy
   c. Communism focuses on class differences rather than racial differences
   d. they favored state ownership of property

   4. _____

5. Roosevelt's Executive Order issued on June 25, 1941,
   a. outlawed discrimination in defense industries
   b. provided for black membership in labor unions
   c. gave work to unemployed black writers
   d. banned discrimination in the armed forces

   5. _____

6. Which of the following was *not* one of the problems African American writers faced?
   a. White readers expected black racial stereotypes.
   b. Black readers wished idealized versions of black life.
   c. Black writers wished to be judged by a single standard of criticism.
   d. White critics would not review black writers' work.

   6. _____

7. The depiction of everyday life and speech of ordinary people is called
   a. social protest
   b. propaganda
   c. naturalism
   d. realism

   7. _____

8. The precise depiction of environmental and social conditions is called
   a. social protest
   b. propaganda
   c. naturalism
   d. realism

   8. _____

9. The form chosen by poets to reconcile social protest and literary requirements was
   a. free verse
   b. the sonnet
   c. rhymed couplets
   d. blank verse

   9. _____

10. Which of the following pairs is *not* correct?
    a. Margaret Walker: "Southern Mansion"
    b. Arna Bontemps: "A Black Man Talks of Reaping"
    c. Margaret Walker: "For My People"
    d. Sterling A. Brown: "Strange Legacies"

    10. _____

NAME _____ CLASS _____ DATE _____

SCORE _____

Sterling A. Brown
Strange Legacies

Text page 391

An Open-Book Test

A. Understanding Ideas and Poetic Techniques

Write the letter of the best answer to each question. (10 points each)

1. The speaker admires Jack Johnson for all of the following *except*
   a. taking punishment   c. his confidence
   b. his sense of humor   d. his grin   1. _____

2. The word *Brother* in line 16 refers to
   a. Jack Johnson   c. John Henry
   b. Jim Jeffries   d. the reader   2. _____

3. What does the speaker mean by "what we need now" in line 21?
   a. Greater naturalness   c. Resistance
   b. Social protest   d. Perseverance   3. _____

4. The subject of the verb *have seen* in lines 31 and 33 is
   a. *Who*, line 28
   b. *couple*, line 27
   c. *floods*, line 28
   d. *Red River Bottom*, line 27   4. _____

5. The hardships faced by Southern farmers included all of the following
   except
   a. floods   b. drought   c. fires   d. epidemics   5. _____

6. Who is speaking in lines 40–41?
   a. John Henry   c. Jack Johnson
   b. The nameless couple   d. The narrator   6. _____

7. Which of the following statements about the poem is *not* accurate?
   a. The poem uses rhyme.
   b. The poem uses alliteration.
   c. The poem uses repetition.
   d. The poem uses only standard English.   7. _____

B. Vocabulary

Each of the following italicized words appears in the poem. Choose the best definition for each italicized word. (10 points each)

8. A *legacy* is
   a. a souvenir
   b. a recollection
   c. something handed down from the past
   d. a bequest in a will

   8. _____

9. A smile that is *spacious* is
   a. wide   c. barely visible
   b. comical   d. brief

   9. _____

10. When one *routs* fear,
    a. one increases it
    b. one faces it
    c. one hides from it
    d. one drives it out

    10. _____

Arna Bontemps

Text pages 396–408

A. Understanding Ideas and Poetic Techniques

Write the letter of the best answer to each question. (5 points each)

1. In "A Black Man Talks of Reaping," the speaker fears
   a. his lands will be flooded
   b. he will not be able to sell his crop
   c. his children will leave the farm
   d. the grain will be taken by birds or by the wind

   1. _____

2. How does the speaker try to assure a good harvest?
   a. He plants a great deal of seed.
   b. He plants beside rivers.
   c. He plants in Canada and in Mexico.
   d. He plants in his neighbors' fields.

   2. _____

3. What are his children forced to do?
   a. They gather stalks and roots in the fields.
   b. They collect grain that has been left in fields reaped by others.
   c. They have to eat unripe fruit.
   d. They must find other fields to sow.

   3. _____

4. In "Southern Mansion," the setting includes
   a. cypress trees   c. weeping willows
   b. live oaks   d. poplars

   4. _____

5. The ghosts in the poem include all of the following *except*
   a. Southern gentlemen   c. Southern cavalry
   b. Southern ladies   d. Southern slaves

   5. _____

6. The sounds in the poem include all of the following *except*
   a. music   c. a tinkling in the field
   b. groans   d. an iron clank

   6. _____

B. Understanding the Short Story

Write the letter of the best answer to each questions. (5 points each)

7. At the opening of the story, Jeff Patton has difficulty
   a. putting on his bow tie   c. lacing his shoes
   b. brushing his swallow-tailed coat   d. shaving

   7. _____

8. Jennie uses a cane because
   a. her joints are stiff
   b. she is blind
   c. she is recovering from a broken leg
   d. she has dizzy spells

   8. _____

9. What has happened to most of Jeff's chickens?
   a. They have been sold.
   b. They have eaten poison.
   c. He has given them away.
   d. They have been killed or stolen.

   9. _____

10. The crop that Jeff and his neighbors grow is
    a. wheat   b. corn   c. cotton   d. potatoes

    10. _____

11. Jeff has changed in several ways. Which of the following is *not* one of the changes?
    a. He talks to himself.
    b. He can no longer feed himself.
    c. He has lapses of memory.
    d. He is terrified by unfamiliar sounds.

    11. _____

12. Jeff's condition has been caused by
    a. a fall from a horse
    b. an automobile accident
    c. a paralytic stroke
    d. fatigue

    12. _____

C. Vocabulary

Choose the best synonym or definition for each italicized word. (8 points each)

13. A *grimace* is an expression of
    a. pain or annoyance
    b. confusion
    c. slyness
    d. amusement

    13. _____

14. Something or someone that is *obstinate* is
    a. flexible
    b. difficult to control
    c. generous and considerate
    d. open to new ideas

    14. _____

15. An *ordeal* is
    a. a violent disturbance
    b. a painful or trying experience
    c. a mysterious occurrence
    d. a punishment for wrongdoing

    15. _____

16. One becomes *tremulous* when one is
    a. frightened   b. happy   c. sleepy   d. disorderly

    16. _____

17. One can *suppress*
    a. time   b. shelter   c. emotion   d. food

    17. _____

Richard Wright
from **Black Boy**

Text page 412

A. Understanding Main Ideas

Write the letter of the best answer to each question. (10 points each)

1. Wright began writing a story because
   a. he wanted to impress his classmates
   b. he had nothing better to do
   c. he couldn't find a job
   d. he hoped to become a famous writer   1. _____

2. When Wright's classmates saw his story in the newspaper,
   a. they congratulated him on his success
   b. they asked to see the next installment
   c. they accused him of copying it
   d. they treated him with new respect   2. _____

3. The aspect of Wright's story that caused the most comment was
   a. its title
   b. its length
   c. its division into three parts
   d. its made-up plot   3. _____

4. Wright's mother was afraid that the story would affect Wright's chances of
   a. getting a scholarship
   b. running for public office
   c. being promoted from eighth grade
   d. getting a job as a teacher   4. _____

5. At the age of fifteen, Wright had made up his mind
   a. to achieve a fortune through get-rich-quick schemes
   b. to become a newspaper editor
   c. to leave Mississippi for the North
   d. to get a college education   5. _____

B. Vocabulary

Each of the following sentences contains an italicized word that appears in the selection. Choose the best synonym for each italicized word. (10 points each)

6. Wright's classmates were *baffled* when they read his story in the newspaper.
   a. angry   **b.** satisfied   **c.** confused   **d.** jealous

   6. _____

7. His uncle's attitude toward the story was *contemptuous*.
   a. sad   **b.** scornful   **c.** amused   **d.** serious

   7. _____

8. Wright felt that the North *symbolized* hope
   a. represented   **c.** remained
   b. became   **d.** resembled

   8. _____

9. He felt that his ambitions were being *stifled*.
   a. held back   **c.** shaped
   b. encouraged   **d.** misunderstood

   9. _____

10. Wright told no one about his *ultimate* dreams.
    a. secret   **b.** earliest   **c.** happiest   **d.** highest

    10. _____

C. Essay

Choose one of the following topics for a brief essay. Refer to the selection as often as you wish.

1. "From no quarter, with the exception of the Negro newspaper editor, had there come a single encouraging word." Explain why Wright was disappointed by the reactions to his story.

2. Wright says that in trying to make something of himself, he was "pushing against the current of my environment." What obstacles did he find in his drive for recognition?

Richard Wright
The Man Who Was Almost a Man

Text page 420

A. Understanding Main Ideas

Write the letter of the best answer to each question. (10 points each)

1. Why does Dave stop at Joe's store?
   a. He wants to look at a catalog.
   b. He needs to borrow money.
   c. He is picking up groceries.
   d. He has to replace a broken tool.   1. _____

2. At supper, all of the following foods are served *except*
   a. cornbread
   b. salad greens
   c. black-eyed peas
   d. buttermilk   2. _____

3. What is Dave's job?
   a. He plows land for Jim Hawkins.
   b. He cleans out Hawkins's barn.
   c. He takes care of Hawkins's stable.
   d. He is a hired hand for several plantation owners.   3. _____

4. To get money from his mother, Dave uses several strategies. Which of
   the following is *not* one of them?
   a. He claims that the family needs a gun in the house.
   b. He offers to help her around the house.
   c. He promises to bring the gun for his father.
   d. He tells his mother that he loves her.   4. _____

5. After Dave confesses to shooting the mule,
   a. his mother begs Hawkins to forgive him
   b. Hawkins asks Dave for the gun
   c. Dave offers to work for nothing to pay for the mule
   d. Dave's father tells him to return the gun and give the money to Hawkins   5. _____

6. Dave runs away from home for several reasons. Which of the following is *not* one of them?

    a. He is afraid of being beaten by his father.

    b. He has been humiliated by the crowd's laughter.

    c. He wants to make people sorry for the way they have treated him.

    d. He resents having to pay for the dead mule.

    6. _____

B. Vocabulary

Choose the best synonym for each of the following italicized words.
(10 points each)

7. After Dave talks to Joe, he feels *elated*.

    a. confident   **b.** nervous   **c.** proud   **d.** happy

    7. _____

8. Dave tries to *muster* courage to speak to his mother.

    a. create   **b.** pretend   **c.** gather   **d.** demand

    8. _____

9. When Dave grabs for Jenny's mane, she *flinches*.

    a. snorts   **c.** shudders

    b. whirls   **d.** draws back

    9. _____

10. Dave holds the gun *gingerly*.

    a. carefully   **c.** confidently

    b. longingly   **d.** tightly

    10. _____

C. Essay

Write a brief essay on the following topic.

Discuss Wright's attitude toward Dave Saunders. In your opinion, is Wright sympathetic to this seventeen-year-old boy who wants desperately to be a man, or is he critical of Dave's immaturity and lack of responsibility? Support your opinion with evidence from the story.

Chester Himes
Black Laughter

Text page 433

A. Understanding Main Ideas

Write the letter of the best answer to each question. (10 points each)

1. The checkroom attendant
   a. waits for Bubber to give her a tip
   b. refuses to check the couple's coats
   c. looks angry when Bubber approaches
   d. tells Bubber's girl friend to keep her coat

   1. _____

2. After Bubber and his girl friend are seated,
   a. Bubber tries to control his frustration
   b. Bubber asks for a different table
   c. the girl orders fried chicken
   d. Bubber glares at the people sitting at the next table

   2. _____

3. On the dance floor,
   a. Bubber and his date chat casually
   b. Bubber and his girl friend do not look at each other
   c. white couples stare at Bubber
   d. Bubber's girl friend smiles at the orchestra leader

   3. _____

4. Which of the following does *not* take place during the floor show?
   a. Bubber and his girl friend pretend to be amused.
   b. Bubber and his girl friend quarrel.
   c. Bubber explains the comedians' jokes to the girl.
   d. Bubber and his girl friend eat their dinner in silence.

   4. _____

5. The waiter's attitude is
   a. brusque   c. friendly
   b. hostile   d. sullen

   5. _____

B. Vocabulary

Choose the best synonym for each italicized word. (10 points each)

6. The people at the next table give the girl a *furtive* look.
   a. stealthy   **b.** scornful   **c.** hasty   **d.** silly

   6. _____

7. Bubber and his partner do *intricate* steps to the dance music.
   a. well-rehearsed   **c.** interesting
   b. complex   **d.** careful

   7. _____

8. Bubber finds his anger *stifling*.
   a. mounting   **c.** ending
   b. threatening   **d.** suffocating

   8. _____

9. The girl treats the waiter with *disdain*.
   a. respect   **c.** contempt
   b. annoyance   **d.** disinterest

   9. _____

10. Bubber's voice sounds *jubilant*.
    a. tense   **b.** joyful   **c.** serious   **d.** furious

    10. _____

C. Essay

Write a brief essay on this topic.

A plot summary tells what happens in a story and also explains its structure. It identifies the main conflict, tells how the conflict develops, and gives its outcome. Write a plot summary of "Black Laughter."

Margaret Walker

Text pages 442–447

An Open-Book Test

A. Understanding Ideas and Poetic Techniques

Write the letter of the best answer to each question. (10 points each)

1. All of the following places are mentioned in "For My People" *except*
   a. Chicago   **c.** New Orleans
   b. Baltimore   **d.** New York   1. _____

2. In "For My People," alliteration appears in all of the following *except*
   a. line 1   **c.** line 4
   b. line 3   **d.** line 8   2. _____

3. The music referred to in "For My People" includes all of the following except
   a. spirituals   **c.** laments
   b. blues   **d.** ragtime   3. _____

4. In "For My People," people's lives are cut short by all of the following *except*
   a. overwork   **c.** a blood disorder
   b. tuberculosis   **d.** mob violence   4. _____

5. In "Lineage," the author uses all of the following devices *except*
   a. parallelism   **c.** internal rhyme
   b. alliteration   **d.** repetition   5. _____

6 In structure, "Childhood" is similar to
   a. free verse   **c.** a ballad
   b. a sonnet   **d.** a blues song   6. _____

7. Which of the following pairs in "Childhood" do *not* match?
   a. Imperfect rhyme: lines 5 and 8
   b. Personification: lines 1–2
   c. Alliteration: line 9
   d. Perfect rhyme: lines 13–14   7. _____

B. Vocabulary

Choose the best synonym or definition for each italicized word. (5 points each)

8. A *dirge* is best described as
   a. a simple song
   b. a song of congratulation
   c. a hymn
   d. a sad song   8. _____

9. To be *dispossessed* is
   a. to feel depressed
   b. to be misrepresented
   c. to have one's property taken away
   d. to lose one's job   9. _____

10. Those who are *omniscient* are
    a. all-powerful   c. oppressors
    b. all-knowing   d. pious   10. _____

11. People who *flounder*
    a. move confusedly
    b. are held back by force
    c. struggle to succeed
    d. creep face downward   11. _____

12. A *leech* is
    a. a an insect
    b. a person that lives at the expense of others
    c. a creature that lives in interdependence with another
    d. a money-hungry individual   12. _____

13. When one *undermines* an argument, one
    a. supports it   c. questions it
    b. emphasizes it   d. weakens it   13. _____

C. Essay

Write a paraphrase of "Lineage" or "Childhood," restating the poem's ideas in your own words.

Analogy Test 5

Recognizing Relationships in Verbal Analogies

Write the letter of the best answer to each question. (10 points each)

1. loam : soil :: poplar : _____
   a. tree   b. leaf   c. seed   d. fruit

   1. _____

2. scrawny : frame :: grotesque : _____
   a. ugly   b. appearance   c. boniness   d. beautiful

   2. _____

3. tolerate : endure :: contend : _____
   a. opponent   b. strength   c. struggle   d. fighter

   3. _____

4. crudely : atmospheric :: intolerably : _____
   a. semblance   c. stupor
   b. monotonously   d. dull

   4. _____

5. cavernous : vast :: contemptuous : _____
   a. variable   b. scornful   c. huge   d. alien

   5. _____

6. conceivable : inconceivable :: facile : _____
   a. easy   c. difficult
   b. straightforward   d. unbelievable

   6. _____

7. sinuous : movement :: staccato : _____
   a. laugh   b. turn   c. moment   d. poise

   7. _____

8. beckoning : chiding :: prolonged : _____
   a. prolonging   c. lengthy
   b. adjoining   d. collided

   8. _____

9. anguish : suffering :: taboo : _____
   a. voodoo   c. agony
   b. prohibition   d. drawing

   9. _____

10. surge : serge :: knot : _____
    a. not   b. knife   c. group   d. well

    10. _____

CONTEMPORARY
AFRICAN AMERICAN LITERATURE
Introduction

Units 7–10

Text page 453

Understanding Main Ideas

Write the letter of the best answer to each question. (10 points each)

1. The publication of *Native Son* in 1940 had a number of effects. Which of
   the following was *not* one of them?
   a. The book became a bestseller.
   b. The book conveyed an optimistic view of the relations between black
   and white Americans.
   c. The novel revealed many truths about racism in the United States.
   d. Wright's book changed the character of African American literature.

   1. _____

2. The new form of music developed by black musicians during the 1940s
   was
   a. Dixieland   **c.** bebop
   b. jazz   **d.** ragtime

   2. _____

3. Which of the following pairs is *not* correct?
   a. Chester Himes: *If He Hollers Let Him Go*
   b. Ralph Ellison: *Invisible Man*
   c. Richard Wright: *Black Boy*
   d. Ann Petry: *Annie Allen*

   3. _____

4. Which of the following statements is *not* accurate?
   a. The Brown decision declared segregation in all public areas
   unconstitutional.
   b. In the Brown decision, the defending party was a segregated public
   school in Topeka, Kansas.
   c. In the Brown decision, the Supreme Court relied on the testimony of
   psychologists.
   d. In the Brown decision, the Supreme Court held that segregation in
   educational facilities was unconstitutional.

   4. _____

5. Which of these pairs is *not* correct?
   a. Martin Luther King, Jr.: Southern Christian Leadership Conference
   b. Stokely Carmichael: Student Nonviolent Coordinating Committee
   c. Marcus Garvey: National Association for the Advancement of Colored
   People
   d. James Farmer: Congress of Racial Equality

   5. _____

6. Malcolm X is associated with
   a. the March on Washington for Jobs and Freedom
   b. the National Urban League
   c. the Black Arts Movement
   d. the concept of Black Power

6. _____

7. In 1965, Watts, Los Angeles, was the scene of
   a. a race riot
   b. a peaceful demonstration for civil rights
   c. a gathering of civil rights organizations
   d. the assassination of a popular African American leader

7. _____

8. Which of the following pairs is *not* correct?
   a. James Baldwin: *Notes of a Native Son*
   b. LeRoi Jones: *The Fire Next Time*
   c. Claude Brown: *Manchild in the Promised Land*
   d. Anne Moody: *Coming of Age in Mississippi*

8. _____

9. During the 1970s, emphasis in African American literature shifted from poetry to
   a. drama   **c.** oratory
   b. fiction   **d.** nonfiction

9. _____

10. Contemporary African American novelists include all of the following *except*
   a. Toni Morrison   **c.** Gloria Naylor
   b. Alice Walker   **d.** Rita Dove

10. _____

CONTEMPORARY SHORT STORIES
James Baldwin
The Rockpile

Unit Seven

Text page 473

A. Understanding Main Ideas

Write the letter of the best answer to each question. (10 points each)

1. Roy and John are not allowed to play on the rockpile because
   a. it is too far away from where they live
   b. nobody else in the neighborhood is allowed to play there
   c. their parents know it is a dangerous place to play
   d. Aunt Florence forbids them to play there   1. _____

2. Roy goes downstairs to play because
   a. John encourages him to go
   b. Aunt Florence is coming to visit
   c. his mother is not watching him
   d. he wants to anger his father   2. _____

3. How does Gabriel react to Roy's injury?
   a. He becomes angry at Roy.
   b. He becomes angry at his wife.
   c. He forgives John.
   d. He forgives his wife.   3. _____

4. What is John's relationship to Gabriel?
   a. He is Gabriel's son by a previous marriage.
   b. He is Gabriel's younger son.
   c. He is Gabriel's stepson.
   d. He is Gabriel's firstborn.   4. _____

5. Which of the following statements about the story is *not* correct?
   a. John tries to keep Roy from leaving the house.
   b. Gabriel blames John for Roy's accident.
   c. Elizabeth tries to shield John from Gabriel's anger.
   d. Gabriel scolds Roy for disobeying his mother.   5. _____

B. Vocabulary

Each of the following sentences contains an italicized word that appears in the selection. Choose the best synonym for each italicized word. (10 points each)

6. Roy is more *reckless* than John.
    a. timid   **c.** daring
    b. obedient   **d.** studious   **6.** _____

7. The boys on the rockpile *grapple* with each other.
    a. joke   **c.** wrestle
    b. fight   **d.** rejoice   **7.** _____

8. Elizabeth and her sons wait for Gabriel with *apprehension.*
    a. enthusiasm   **c.** reluctance
    b. impatience   **d.** dread   **8.** _____

9. Elizabeth's excuses begin to *exasperate* Gabriel.
    a. worry   **c.** excite
    b. irritate   **d.** bore   **9.** _____

10. Roy *recoil*s when his father touches his forehead.
    a. draws back   **c.** runs away
    b. screams out   **d.** faints   **10.** _____

C. Essay

Choose one of the following topics for a brief essay. You can refer to the story as often as you wish.

1. Do you think Gabriel is "fair" in his reaction to Roy's injury? Why doesn't he blame Roy? Give reasons for your answer.

2. Using examples from the story, describe John's character. Why doesn't he try harder to restrain his brother? Why doesn't he respond when Gabriel questions him?

Eugenia W. Collier
Marigolds

Text page 485

A. Understanding Main Ideas

Write the letter of the best answer to each question. (10 points each)

1. The marigolds remind the narrator of
   a. her mother's garden
   b. a painful experience
   c. a difficult school year
   d. a long, cold winter

   1. _____

2. The children liked to tease Miss Lottie because she
   a. enjoyed chasing them
   b. had more money than they had
   c. lived in a fine house
   d. was easily angered

   2. _____

3. Who led the children's attack on Miss Lottie's marigolds?
   a. Joey   c. Lizabeth
   b. John Burke   d. Maybelle

   3. _____

4. When Lizabeth overheard her father crying, she felt
   a. anger and scorn
   b. annoyance at his weakness
   c. bewilderment and fear
   d. sympathy for her mother

   4. _____

5. To Miss Lottie, the marigolds represented
   a. a way to keep herself busy during the long, hot summer
   b. a challenge to the children in the neighborhood
   c. a patch of beauty in the midst of ugliness
   d. something pretty for her son to look at

   5. _____

B. Vocabulary

Each of the following sentences contains an italicized word that appears in the selection. Choose the best synonym for each italicized word. (10 points each)

6. A strange sense of *nostalgia* comes over the narrator when she thinks of Miss Lottie's marigolds.
   a. yearning toward the future
   b. disappointment over past events
   c. longing for the past
   d. contentment with present life   6. _____

7. Miss Lottie lived in a *ramshackle* house.
   a. rickety   c. spacious
   b. well-built   d. tiny   7. _____

8. Lizabeth felt sad after her *malicious* attack on Miss Lottie's flowers.
   a. frenzied   c. destructive
   b. joyful   d. spiteful   8. _____

9. Her parents' conversation was *audible*.
   a. extremely loud   c. filled with emotion
   b. difficult to follow   d. capable of being heard   9. _____

10. Lizabeth felt *compassion* for Miss Lottie.
    a. a sense of hatred   c. sorrow
    b. pity   d. love   10. _____

C. Essay

Choose one of the following topics for a brief essay. You can refer to the story as often as you wish.

1. Why do you think Miss Lottie never replanted her marigold patch? Do you think the marigold incident would have been less memorable for Lizabeth if Miss Lottie had replanted her garden?

2. Explain what the narrator means when she says "And I too have planted marigolds." Before you write, reread the passages that describe the marigolds—their significance for Miss Lottie and their significance for the narrator.

Paule Marshall
To Da-duh, in Memoriam

Text page 499

A. Understanding Main Ideas

Write the letter of the best answer to each question. (10 points each)

1. The setting of this story is
   a. a large Caribbean island within recent times
   b. the West Indies during the Second World War
   c. a West Indies island while it was still a colony of Great Britain
   d. a town in Panama

   1. _____

2. Da-duh introduces the narrator to different trees, including all of the following *except*
   a. chestnut   c. papaw
   b. royal palm   d. breadfruit

   2. _____

3. At first, the narrator's stories about New York
   a. intrigue Da-duh   c. make Da-duh sad
   b. bore Da-duh   d. displease Da-duh

   3. _____

4. The narrator entertains her grandmother in all of the following ways *except*
   a. singing popular songs
   b. describing modern conveniences
   c. reading to her from the Bible
   d. performing dances

   4. _____

5. The narrator promises that she will send Da-duh
   a. a postcard of the Empire State Building
   b. a record album
   c. money to come to New York
   d. a photograph of her class at school

   5. _____

B. Vocabulary

Each of the following sentences contains an italicized word that appears in the selection. Choose the best synonym for each italicized word. (10 points each)

6. Before meeting Da-duh, the narrator had considered her mother to be *formidable*.
   a. dignified
   b. awesome
   c. stern
   d. fortunate

   6. _____

7. The narrator describes herself as a *truculent* child.
   a. defiant
   b. thoughtful
   c. morose
   d. pretty

   7. _____

8. Da-duh lived in a *perennial* summer kingdom.
   a. beautiful
   b. lonely
   c. perpetual
   d. monotonous

   8. _____

9. Da-duh became increasingly *dispirited*.
   a. weak
   b. dejected
   c. curious
   d. frustrated

   9. _____

10. Her grandmother wore a dress that was *austere*.
    a. severe and simple
    b. old-fashioned
    c. made of shiny material
    d. very long

    10. _____

C. Essay

Choose one of the following topics for a brief essay. You can refer to the story as often as you wish.

1. Have you ever heard from a friend or relative, or read somewhere, about a way of life or culture that is very different from your own? How did the account make you feel—frightened? or envious? or glad that you live where you do? Describe your reaction.

2. At the end of the story, the narrator says that she has always lived "within the shadow of her [grandmother's] death." Do you think she feels responsible for Da-duh's death? Do you think she *was* responsible? Explain.

Ernest J. Gaines
Robert Louis Stevenson Banks, aka Chimley

Text page 513

A. Understanding Main Ideas

Write the letter of the best answer to each question. (10 points each)

1. In the community where Chimley and Mat live, Mathu has a reputation for
   a. catching the most perches
   b. being a sissy
   c. standing up to white people
   d. resisting arrest   1. _____

2. After the fight between Mathu and Fix in front of Marshall's store, the sheriff
   a. rewarded Mathu for winning
   b. drank his pop and ate his gingerbread and did nothing
   c. hit both Mathu and Fix
   d. arrested Mathu   2. _____

3. When Chimley and Mat hear that they are wanted on the Marshall place, they are
   a. excited
   b. annoyed that their fishing has been interrupted
   c. scared
   d. pleased to be included in the action   3. _____

4. From the conversation between the two men, we can infer that, in similar situations in the past, Chimley and Mat
   a. always were eager to help
   b. stood up for each other
   c. stayed underneath their beds until the fight was over
   d. avoided getting involved   4. _____

5. The fact that Mat and Chimley can understand each other without saying very much tells us that
   a. they don't like to talk
   b. they probably speak different dialects
   c. they don't trust each other
   d. they have been friends for a long time   5. _____

B. Vocabulary

Each of the following quotations contains an italicized word or phrase. Choose the word or phrase in standard English that best fits the meaning of the word or words in italics. (10 points each)

6. "Then that oldest boy of Berto, that *sissy* one they called Fue, come running down the riverbank . . ."
   a. courageous
   b. timid
   c. aggressive
   d. ugly

   6. _____

7. "Then he walked up to Mathu, *cracked him 'side the jaw*, and Mathu hit the ground."
   a. cracked his jaw open
   b. slapped him across his face
   c. hit him beneath the chin
   d. struck him on the side of the face

   7. _____

8. "Now, I ain't even stepped in the house good 'fore that old woman started *fussing at me*."
   a. hitting me
   b. nagging me
   b. insulting me
   d. throwing things at me

   8. _____

9. "'What you doing shooting out that window, *raising all that racket* for?'"
   a. raising all that dust
   b. upsetting the neighbors
   c. making all that noise
   d. scaring everyone

   9. _____

10. ". . . she had enough sense *not to get too cute*."
    a. not to look too pretty
    b. not to stop talking
    c. not to flirt with me
    d. not to get smart with me

    10. _____

C. Essay

Write a brief essay on this topic. Refer to the story as often as you wish.

Discuss the characters of Mat and Chimley as they are revealed in this story. What do these men have in common? What methods are used to characterize them? What do you learn about Chimley from the scene with his wife?

William Melvin Kelley
Brother Carlyle

Text page 521

A. Understanding Main Ideas

Write the letter of the best answer to each question. (10 points each)

1. What is the reason Mance gives for not objecting to the fire?
   a. It was cold out.
   b. His brother was punishing him.
   c. He wanted to impress the members of Carlyle's club.
   d. All the boys were taking turns.

   1. _____

2. From the conversation between husband and wife, we learn that
   a. Mr. Bedlow usually works late
   b. Carlyle has played mean pranks on Mance before
   c. Mance is the father's favorite child
   d. Mr. and Mrs. Bedlow never argue

   2. _____

3. When Mr. Bedlow gives the boys money,
   a. they share it equally
   b. Mance spends all his money foolishly
   c. Carlyle spends all the money on a gift for himself
   d. Carlyle and Mance buy a cowboy costume for their father

   3. _____

4. The words that best describe Mance's feelings toward Carlyle are
   a. jealousy and suspicion   c. affection and loyalty
   b. anger and hatred   d. confusion and dismay

   4. _____

5. How does Mr. Bedlow interpret his wife's concern about the two boys?
   a. He thinks she is right to be alarmed at Carlyle's treatment of Mance.
   b. He thinks she gives the boys too much attention.
   c. He thinks she babies Mance.
   d. He thinks she picks on Mance too much.

   5. _____

B. Vocabulary

Each of the following sentences contains an italicized word that appears in the selection. Choose the best synonym for each italicized word. (10 points each)

6. Smoke from the fire *obscured* Mance's body.
   a. swirled around
   b. blackened
   c. concealed
   d. drifted away from

   6. _____

7. Carlyle always had a *valid* excuse for his behavior.
   a. flimsy
   b. silly
   c. logical
   d. different

   7. _____

8. Her husband often *misconstrued* her words.
   a. believed
   b. was moved by
   c. ignored
   d. misunderstood

   8. _____

9. Mr. Bedlow *stalked* into the living room.
   a. ran awkwardly
   b. walked angrily
   c. strolled leisurely
   d. tiptoed quietly

   9. _____

10. Mance seemed *perplexed* about how the money was spent.
    a. confused
    b. angry
    c. proud
    d. regretful

    10. _____

C. Essay

Write a brief essay on this topic. Refer to the story as often as you wish.

Mrs. Bedlow is clearly concerned about Carlyle's treatment of Mance, but her husband thinks she is overreacting. What do you think? Is this story about the pranks that children normally play on each other, or is the situation more serious? What makes you agree with one character and not the other? Explain.

Diane Oliver
Neighbors

Text page 527

A. Understanding Main Ideas

Write the letter of the best answer to each question. (10 points each)

1. The family's life has been changed in several ways. Which of the following is *not* one of the changes?
   a. The front door is kept closed at all times.
   b. The father's employers are making his job more difficult.
   c. Ellie has had to quit her job.
   d. Cruise cars have been circling the block at night.

   1. _____

2. How does Tommy show that he is frightened?
   a. He reads the Uncle Wiggly book by himself.
   b. He refuses to take his bath.
   c. He bursts into tears when he sees Ellie.
   d. He asks to sleep in his parents' room.

   2. _____

3. Why is Tommy the only black child to be admitted into the all-white school?
   a. He was the only one to take the entrance examination.
   b. The other black families in the community do not wish to get involved.
   c. The school has room for only one new student.
   d. Tommy's family is the only black family in the community.

   3. _____

4. When the father says "somebody's got to be the first one," he means
   a. one white school has to be the first to accept a black
   b. one black child has to be the first to attend a white school
   c. one family has to get its name into the newspapers
   d. one black family has to be the first to have their house patrolled

   4. _____

5. Which member of the family is the last one to resist giving up?
   a. the mother   **c.** the father
   b. Ellie   **d.** Tommy

   5. _____

B. Vocabulary

Each of the following sentences contains an italicized word that appears in the selection. Choose the best synonym for each italicized word. (10 points each)

6. The warmth of the house *permeated* her skin.
   a. burned
   b. irritated
   c. caressed
   d. passed through

   6. _____

7. The noises *accumulated* in the back of her mind.
   a. blended
   b. piled up
   c. roared
   d. became softer

   7. _____

8. The father *instinctively* knocked them to the floor when he heard the blast.
   a. forcefully
   b. gently
   c. spontaneously
   d. deliberately

   8. _____

9. Ellie gave an *involuntary* sigh when she thought about Tommy on his first day of school.
   a. unhappy
   b. anxious
   c. automatic
   d. uneasy

   9. _____

10. Ellie's mother tried to keep her *composure*.
    a. silence
    b. calmness
    c. earthenware
    d. temper

    10. _____

C. Essay

Write a brief essay on this topic. Refer to the story as often as you wish.

How does the author help you to understand the different points of view of the characters in "Neighbors"? How does she convey the attitudes of Ellie's parents, of Ellie, and of Tommy? Do you feel that these varying points of view give you a better grasp of the events that were taking place during the 1960s?

Alice Walker
Everyday Use

Text page 543

A. Understanding Main Ideas

Write the letter of the best answer to each question. (10 points each)

1. Which of the following descriptions best fits Dee?
   a. Sympathetic and generous
   b. Thoughtful and affectionate
   c. Self-centered and confident
   d. Frank and sincere

   1. _____

2. Which of the following statements best describes Maggie's feelings about her sister?
   a. Maggie is ashamed of Dee.
   b. Maggie dislikes her sister intensely.
   c. Maggie feels superior to Dee.
   d. Maggie feels envious and a bit frightened around Dee.

   2. _____

3. Which of these statements accurately describes the point of view of the story?
   a. The story is told in first-person point of view.
   b. The story is told by an all-knowing narrator.
   c. The story is told in limited third-person point of view.
   d. The point of view shifts from first to third person.

   3. _____

4. Which of the following is *not* an accurate description of the setting?
   a. A rundown house in a pasture
   b. A yard of hard clay
   c. A rural area in the South
   d. A patio with an outdoor grill

   4. _____

5. The theme of the story deals with
   a. the meaning of one's heritage
   b. the narrator's struggle to understand her daughters
   c. the competition between two sisters for their mother's approval
   d. the impact of new ideas on old traditions

   5. _____

B. Vocabulary

Choose the best synonym for each of the italicized words. (10 points each)

6. The narrator dreams about *confronting* her daughter on a TV program.
   a. surprising
   b. facing
   c. insulting
   d. embracing

   6. _____

7. In school, Dee had a few *furtive* friends.
   a. secret   b. boastful   c. modest   d. loyal

   7. _____

8. After Jimmy T married a city girl, Dee had to *recompose* herself.
   a. calm   b. blame   c. criticize   d. change

   8. _____

9. Dee snaps pictures of Maggie *cowering* behind her mother.
   a. shifting from one leg to the other
   b. shrinking in fear
   c. covering her face
   d. grinning

   9. _____

10. Dee says she can't stand being named for the people who *oppress* her.
    a. offend   b. annoy   c. hurt   d. persecute

    10. _____

C. Essay

Choose one of these topics for a brief essay.

1. Dee is a complex character who is revealed through direct and indirect characterization. Give your impression of her and support your discussion with evidence from the story.

2. Has the story "Everyday Use" made you think about your own heritage in a new way? Discuss your responses to the story and tell what the word *heritage* means to you.

Reginald McKnight
The Kind of Light That Shines on Texas

Text page 556

A. Understanding Main Ideas

Write the letter of the best answer to each question. (10 points each)

1. Why does Clint dislike Marvin Pruitt?
   a. Marvin picks on him.
   b. Marvin embarrasses him.
   c. Marvin tells racist jokes.
   d. Marvin is friends with Kelvin Oakley.   1. _____

2. How do the students feel about Oakley?
   a. They consider him the class clown.
   b. They look up to him as a leader.
   c. They recognize him as a bully.
   d. They are eager to be his friend.   2. _____

3. Clint doesn't tell his mother about Oakley because
   a. he knows that she doesn't care about his problems
   b. he's afraid she will call up Oakley's parents
   c. he wants to be strong and closemouthed like his father
   d. he has too much homework to do   3. _____

4. How does Clint feel when he thinks about the scene in the locker room?
   a. He feels that he has betrayed both himself and Marvin.
   b. He has a strong desire to fight Oakley.
   c. He wants to make friends with Marvin.
   d. He regrets that he didn't challenge Oakley.   4. _____

5. What is the climax, or most exciting point, of the story?
   a. Clint knocks Oakley down during a murderball game.
   b. Marvin Pruitt settles scores with Oakley.
   c. Oakley threatens Clint in the locker room.
   d. Clint sees Ah-so smiling.   5. _____

B. Vocabulary

Each of the following sentences contains an italicized word that appears in the selection. Choose the best synonym for each italicized word. (10 points each)

6. The white kids would *scrutinize* the black kids in Clint's class.
   - **a.** taunt
   - **b.** terrorize
   - **c.** compliment
   - **d.** inspect

   6. _____

7. Ah-so sat in class *impassively*.
   - **a.** nervously
   - **b.** showing no emotion
   - **c.** silently
   - **d.** with alertness

   7. _____

8. There was nothing *malevolent* about Ah-so.
   - **a.** violent
   - **b.** interesting
   - **c.** evil
   - **d.** nice

   8. _____

9. Oakley *intimidated* Clint.
   - **a.** threatened
   - **b.** liked
   - **c.** complimented
   - **d.** feared

   9. _____

10. The emptiness of the schoolyard made Clint *vulnerable*.
   - **a.** nervous
   - **b.** confident of victory
   - **c.** open to attack
   - **d.** more violent

   10. _____

C. Essay

Write a brief essay on one of the following topics. Refer to the story as often as you wish.

1. McKnight's story takes place in the 1960s, when many public schools in the South were being desegregated. What insight does this story give you into the experiences of students who lived through that period?

2. Discuss the author's characterization of the students and the teacher. Do you feel that these characters are believable? Defend your answer with specific evidence from the story.

Analogy Test 6

Recognizing Relationships in Verbal Analogies

Write the letter of the best answer to each question. (10 points each)

1. reckless : daring :: jubilant : _____
   a. depressed
   b. joyful
   c. rowdy
   d. ignorant

   1. _____

2. apprehension : calm :: rigid : _____
   a. severity
   b. posture
   c. moving
   d. reliant

   2. _____

3. arid : desert :: ramshackle : _____
   a. palace
   b. pool
   c. field
   d. hut

   3. _____

4. prosperity : wealth :: quest : _____
   a. squalor
   b. search
   c. retribution
   d. reverie

   4. _____

5. status : social :: pressure : _____
   a. atmospheric
   b. stark
   c. funereal
   d. arrogant

   5. _____

6. brisk : walk :: fitful : _____
   a. noise
   b. scrutinize
   c. sleep
   d. fever

   6. _____

7. formidable : awesome :: malicious : _____
   a. spiteful
   b. sympathetic
   c. ferocious
   d. dissonant

   7. _____

8. crevice : small :: protestation : _____
   a. perplexed
   b. enormous
   c. distorted
   d. angry

   8. _____

9. maintain : composure :: treat : _____
   a. intention   **c.** behavior
   b. abrasion   **d.** gift

9. _____

10. queasy : comfortable :: bemused : _____
   a. confused   **c.** clear-headed
   b. vulnerable   **d.** malevolent

10. _____

CONTEMPORARY NONFICTION
Dorothy West
Rachel

Unit Eight

Text page 587

A. Understanding Main Ideas

Write the letter of the best answer to each question. (10 points each)

1. How did the children react to their mother's death?
   a. They refused to accept her death.
   b. They quarreled over her possessions.
   c. They tried to hide their real feelings.
   d. They felt guilt and shame.

   1. _____

2. The words that best describe Rachel are
   a. strong-willed and high-spirited
   b. authoritative and mean-tempered
   c. unfair and nosey
   d. dissatisfied and demanding

   2. _____

3. The children admired all of the following qualities in Rachel *except*
   a. her ability to laugh   c. her meddling
   b. her bravado   d. her liveliness

   3. _____

4. How did her surroundings affect Dorothy West's desire to write?
   a. Her mother encouraged her to be a writer.
   b. The family tried to change her mind.
   c. She felt that she was living inside a story.
   d. She wrote to escape from all the personalities around her.

   4. _____

5. West's memoir of her mother is best described as
   a. an angry recollection
   b. a tribute
   c. a persuasive essay
   d. an objective biography

   5. _____

B. Vocabulary

Each of the following sentences contains an italicized word that appears in the selection. Choose the best synonym for each italicized word. (10 points each)

6. The children *sparred* with each other continuously.
   - **a.** romped
   - **b.** argued
   - **c.** joked
   - **d.** conspired

   6. _____

7. Rachel West was the *dominant* figure in the family.
   - **a.** most wicked
   - **b.** most intelligent
   - **c.** most influential
   - **d.** most energetic

   7. _____

8. Rachel West had *vitality*.
   - **a.** pride
   - **b.** energy
   - **c.** affection
   - **d.** misfortune

   8. _____

9. The children had *ambivalent* feelings toward their mother.
   - **a.** angry
   - **b.** restrained
   - **c.** powerful
   - **d.** conflicting

   9. _____

10. One by one, the children became *disciples* of their mother.
    - **a.** followers
    - **b.** imitations
    - **c.** critics
    - **d.** extensions

    10. _____

C. Essay

Write a brief essay on this topic.

West says that her mother often remarked that speech was given to people in order to hide their thoughts. In your opinion, do people use speech to hide what they're thinking? Do you think this is a good use for speech? Or do you think that people should always say what they are thinking? Explain.

Ralph Ellison
from An Extravagance of Laughter

Text page 593

A. Understanding Main Ideas

Write the letter of the best answer to each question. (10 points each)

1. How does Ellison collect his impressions of New Yorkers?
   a. He reads a great many books.
   b. He takes public transportation all over the city.
   c. He takes the subway around Harlem.
   d. He drives around the borough of Manhattan.

   1. _____

2. A "five o'clock foot race" that the narrator observes involves
   a. a horse race at Belmont
   b. a shoving match on a subway platform
   c. fare jumpers at a subway turnstile
   d. a contest for an empty seat

   2. _____

3. The narrator thinks that the best position in a bus is
   a. a window seat
   b. the front of the bus
   c. the back of the bus
   d. the driver's seat

   3. _____

4. Which statement best describes Ellison's conflict in choosing a bus seat?
   a. He has to choose between a symbol of freedom and his own comfort.
   b. He has to choose between exercising his legs and being too cramped.
   c. He has to choose between sitting among white passengers or remaining with black passengers.
   d. He has to decide whether to be squeezed in the front or squeezed in the back.

   4. _____

5. Ellison admits that he would rather live in
   a. Alabama
   b. a black neighborhood
   c. a white neighborhood
   d. a place without any buses

   5. _____

B. Vocabulary

Each of the following sentences contains an italicized word that appears in the selection. Choose the best synonym for each italicized word. (10 points each)

6. Ellison contrasts the whites he *encounters* in the North with the whites in the South.
   a. bumps into
   b. rides with
   c. meets
   d. jostles

   6. _____

7. Ellison enters the North with a Southern *perspective.*
   a. background with which to evaluate experience
   b. family background
   c. background of genteel manners
   d. habit of judging people

   7. _____

8. The woman on the train had a more *ruthless* stride than the man.
   a. vigorous
   b. relentless
   c. comical
   d. elegant

   8. _____

9. Ellison values his *anonymity* while exploring the city.
   a. independence
   b. cultural identification
   c. private experience
   d. namelessness

   9. _____

10. Ellison notes that sometimes a misunderstood gesture can lead to a *lethal* conflict.
    a. lengthy
    b. disastrous
    c. deadly
    d. massive

    10. _____

C. Essay

Write a brief essay on this topic. Refer to the selection as often as you wish.

Explain Ellison's feelings of irony when he rides the buses in New York. The irony leads to his conflict over where to sit on the bus. Which choice do you think he makes, judging from the tone of this essay?

James Baldwin
My Dungeon Shook

Text page 601

A. Understanding Main Ideas

Write the letter of the best answer to each question. (10 points each)

1. This letter is primarily about
   a. the relationship between James Baldwin and his nephew
   b. the relationship between blacks and whites in America
   c. the relationship between Baldwin and his grandfather
   d. the relationship between Baldwin and his brother

   1. _____

2. Baldwin says that his nephew's future is limited because
   a. he has no ambition
   b. his father has restricted him all his life
   c. white people have set up limits and rules for blacks
   d. he lives in Harlem

   2. _____

3. According to Baldwin, whites are trapped in history because
   a. they have not yet learned to accept blacks
   b. they have never studied the history of their country
   c. they are innocent of any wrongdoing
   d. they trust only in experience

   3. _____

4. The advice Baldwin gives his nephew is
   a. to get a college education
   b. to accept and love white people
   c. to resist change
   d. to try to become like white people

   4. _____

5. Why does Baldwin say that "the country is celebrating one hundred years of freedom one hundred years too soon"?
   a. Many African Americans are still born in ghettos.
   b. The goals of the Emancipation Proclamation have not yet been achieved.
   c. The country is not one hundred years old yet.
   d. African Americans have still not accepted their heritage.

   5. _____

B. Vocabulary

Each of the following sentences contains an italicized word that appears in the selection. Choose the best synonym for each italicized word. (10 points each)

6. James is moody and *vulnerable*.
   a. dejected
   b. capable of being hurt
   c. impertinent
   d. easily angered

   6. _____

7. Baldwin believes that racial hatred has *devastated* the country.
   a. taken over
   b. transformed
   c. ruined
   d. unified

   7. _____

8. Baldwin tells his nephew not to settle for *mediocrity*.
   a. tolerance
   b. oppression
   c. easy compromise
   d. inferior performance

   8. _____

9. Baldwin says any *upheaval* in the universe attacks one's sense of reality.
   a. movement
   b. violent change
   c. explosion
   d. disintegration

   9. _____

10. Baldwin says that the dignity of blacks is *unassailable*.
    a. monumental
    b. profoundly moving
    c. undeniable
    d. vulnerable

    10. _____

C. Essay

Choose one of the following topics for a brief essay. You can refer to the selection as often as you wish.

1. Pretend that you are Baldwin's nephew and respond to your uncle's letter. Comment on Baldwin's feelings and his ideas. Does the letter make you, as James, angry? sad? grateful?

2. Explain what Baldwin is predicting will happen when he quotes these lines: "The very time I thought I was lost, My dungeon shook and my chains fell off." What do you think the dungeon represents? What will cause the dungeon to shake? Whose chains will fall off?

Malcolm X
from **The Autobiography of Malcolm X**

Text page 609

A. Understanding Main Ideas

Write the letter of the best answer to each question. (10 points each)

1. Malcolm X first wanted to educate himself so he could write
   a. to Bimbi
   b. in his diary
   c. for a pardon
   d. to Elijah Muhammad   1. _____

2. Besides copying the dictionary, Malcolm X educated himself
   a. through his visitors
   b. by talking to the other inmates
   c. by reading books from the library
   d. by taking correspondence courses   2. _____

3. The inmates in the Norfolk Prison Colony who gained fame were
   a. the outstanding athletes
   b. Malcolm X and Bimbi
   c. the library aides
   d. the well-read debaters   3. _____

4. What did Malcolm X do when lights were turned out?
   a. He read by a light in the corridor.
   b. He used a flashlight to read by.
   c. He went immediately to sleep.
   d. He tried to remember what he had read during the day.   4. _____

5. Judging from this selection, the word that most accurately describes
   Malcolm X is
   a. humble
   b. ambitious
   c. determined
   d. restless   5. _____

B. Vocabulary

Each of the following sentences contains an italicized word that appears in the selection. Choose the best synonym for each italicized word. (10 points each)

6. Malcolm X's goal was to become *articulate*.
   a. well-read
   b. capable of expressing himself
   c. famous
   d. anonymous   6. _____

7. Malcolm X tried to *emulate* Bimbi.
   a. outdo   c. imitate
   b. sympathize with   d. teach   7. _____

8. He *riffled* the pages noisily.
   a. ripped   c. scribbled on
   b. crumpled   d. thumbed through   8. _____

9. After broadening his word base, it was *inevitable* that Malcolm X would be able to understand the books he read.
   a. joyful   c. certain
   b. improbable   d. unfortunate   9. _____

10. Malcolm was always *engrossed* in his reading.
    a. careless   c. isolated
    b. absorbed   d. critical   10. _____

C. Essay

Write a brief essay on the following topic. Refer to the selection as often as you wish.

Give your impression of Malcolm X, using evidence from his autobiography to support your conclusions. Consider his tone as well as the incidents he chooses to tell about his rehabilitation.

Martin Luther King, Jr.
I Have a Dream

Text page 616

A. Understanding Main Ideas

Write the letter of the best answer to each question. (10 points each)

1. King delivered this speech
   a. to Congress
   b. at the Lincoln Memorial
   c. on the steps of the White House
   d. in front of the Washington Monument

   1. _____

2. The March on Washington was organized in order to
   a. campaign for jobs
   b. increase black voter registration in the South
   c. urge Congress to pass civil rights legislation
   d. get President Kennedy to sign a civil rights bill

   2. _____

3. King warns his audience against the use of
   a. creative protest
   b. physical violence
   c. soul force
   d. dignity and discipline

   3. _____

4. In his speech, King refers to all of the following *except*
   a. the Magna Carta
   b. the Emancipation Proclamation
   c. the Constitution
   d. the Declaration of Independence

   4. _____

5. "*Now* is the time to rise from the dark and desolate valley of segregation to the sunlit path of racial justice." This quotation illustrates all of the following techniques *except*
   a. metaphor
   b. alliteration
   c. irony
   d. antithesis

   5. _____

B. Vocabulary

Each of the following sentences contains an italicized word that appears in the selection. Choose the best synonym for each italicized word. (10 points each)

6. The Emancipation Proclamation was a *momentous* decree.
   a. very important
   b. well-timed
   c. complex
   d. dramatic

6. _____

7. King calls the Emancipation Proclamation a *beacon* of hope.
   a. test   c. statement
   b. signal   d. promise

7. _____

8. The crowd stood in the *sweltering* heat.
   a. depressing   c. wretched
   b. uncomfortably hot   d. midday

8. _____

9. King does not want the struggle for freedom to *degenerate* into bitterness and hatred.
   a. develop   c. deteriorate
   b. languish   d. lead

9. _____

10. King wishes to transform *discord* into harmony.
   a. violence   c. revolution
   b. harsh disagreement   d. feelings of hopelessness

10. _____

C. Essay

Write a brief essay on the following topic. Refer to King's speech as often as you wish.

King clearly intended his speech to unify rather than to divide the different elements of American society. Find evidence of this purpose in the speech. How does King use American values and ideals to emphasize his vision?

Ishmael Reed
America: The Multinational Society

Text page 624

A. Understanding Main Ideas

Write the letter of the best answer to each question. (10 points each)

1. An example that Reed considers a "blurring of cultural styles" is that of
   a. the computer magazine that has no poetry
   b. American intellectuals who speak an African language
   c. the Puritan community's banning of Christmas
   d. the scribbling in public restrooms

   1. _____

2. By "cultural bouillabaisse," the Yale professor means
   a. a cultural mixture
   b. a creative fish stew
   c. a cultural mess
   d. an unchanging civilization

   2. _____

3. The idea that the North American system of government is derived from Europe has been challenged by
   a. Tsarist dissidents
   b. a Yale professor
   c. Native American historians
   d. Benjamin Franklin

   3. _____

4. According to Reed, the influence of foreign curriculums on the American educational system
   a. has been devastating
   b. has been around for a very long time
   c. is just beginning
   d. ended in the early twentieth century

   4. _____

5. Why does Reed believe that the United States is unique in the world?
   a. It is confused about its identity.
   b. It has always been profoundly affected by European ways.
   c. It is a place where the cultures of the world criss-cross.
   d. It is already the brain of the world.

   5. _____

B. Vocabulary

Each of the following sentences contains an italicized word that appears in the selection. Choose the best synonym for each italicized word. (10 points each)

6. Some members of the audience were *bilingual*.
   a. ostracized
   b. able to speak two languages
   c. arrogant
   d. of varied cultural backgrounds

   6. _____

7. Reed believes that a world that is *homogeneous* would be mediocre.
   a. culturally mixed
   b. diversified
   c. unvaried
   d. insensitive

   7. _____

8. One politician *envisions* that the United States will become the place where advanced information systems are kept.
   a. hopes   c. persuades
   b. denies   d. imagines

   8. _____

9. The United States is a *repository* of many cultures.
   a. storehouse   c. mixture
   b. catalog   d. legacy

   9. _____

10. The influence of different cultural styles is more *prevalent* than people realize.
    a. bizarre   c. imaginative
    b. enterprising   d. common

    10. _____

C. Essay

Write a brief essay on the following topic. Refer to the selection as often as you wish.

The essayist uses many of the techniques that are used by writers of fiction and poetry. For example, Reed uses a simile when he compares the Yale professor to an "old-time southern evangelist." Examine some of the literary devices that Reed uses in his essay. How do these devices help to develop his position?

Henry Louis Gates, Jr.
A Giant Step

Text page 632

A. Understanding Main Ideas

Write the letter of the best answer to each question. (10 points each)

1. Gates was first injured
   a. in the schoolyard
   b. in a football game
   c. during a routine physical examination
   d. while playing tennis

   1. _____

2. The doctor who first treats Gates
   a. tells him that he will never become an athlete
   b. discourages him from going into medicine
   c. asks him a number of questions about science
   d. diagnoses a broken hip

   2. _____

3. According to Gates, his greatest frustration was
   a. spending six weeks in traction
   b. quarreling with his mother
   c. not being able to wear regular shoes
   d. missing out on Wimbledon

   3. _____

4. Why were the doctors reluctant to perform another operation?
   a. The procedure had never been successful.
   b. A new hip would last for only fifteen years.
   c. They felt that surgery could be avoided.
   d. Technology was not yet sufficiently advanced.

   4. _____

5. When Gates looks at his orthopedic shoes after surgery, he feels
   a. disgusted
   b. disloyal
   c. jubilant
   d. angry

   5. _____

B. Vocabulary

Each of the following sentences contains an italicized word that appears in the selection. Choose the best synonym for each italicized word. (10 points each)

6. His *gait* in orthopedic shoes was awkward.
   - **a.** posture
   - **b.** self-consciousness
   - **c.** way of walking
   - **d.** heaviness

   6. _____

7. The pain in his hip did not *abate*.
   - **a.** progress
   - **b.** lessen
   - **c.** intensify
   - **d.** move around

   7. _____

8. The quarreling between mother and son became a kind of *ritual*.
   - **a.** prop
   - **b.** necessity
   - **c.** annoyance
   - **d.** ceremony

   8. _____

9. Gates was *immobilized* by a system of weights and pulleys.
   - **a.** prevented from moving
   - **b.** bored
   - **c.** kept awake
   - **d.** injured

   9. _____

10. The doctor told him that the lift in his heel could be *discreet*.
    - **a.** thick
    - **b.** obvious
    - **c.** inconspicuous
    - **d.** increased

    10. _____

C. Essay

Choose one of the following topics for a brief essay. Refer to the selection as often as you wish.

1. Why is "A Giant Step" an appropriate title for this selection? Explain the title's significance on both a literal and a figurative level.

2. Why do you think the narrator changed his mind and didn't throw away his orthopedic shoes? Why does Gates want to have his old shoes bronzed? What do the shoes represent to him? Explain.

Analogy Test 7

Recognizing Relationships in Verbal Analogies

Choose the letter of the best answer to each question. (10 points each)

1. spar : argue :: chide : _____
   a. rivet   c. flourish
   b. scold   d. gad   1. _____

2. riveting : gaze :: dominant : _____
   a. diehard   c. figure
   b. gospel   d. disciple   2. _____

3. inevitable : uncertain :: remote : _____
   a. lethal   c. improbable
   b. distant   d. close by   3. _____

4. jostled : crowd :: bereaved : _____
   a. encounter   c. saddened
   b. nostalgia   d. death   4. _____

5. massive : tiny :: impertinent : _____
   a. respectful   c. profound
   b. insolent   d. large   5. _____

6. pillar : building :: ghetto : _____
   a. tenement   c. city
   b. poverty   d. perspective   6. _____

7. languish : flourish :: momentous : _____
   a. redemptive   c. occasion
   b. insignificant   d. prodigious   7. _____

8. orator : speech :: disciple : _____
   a. ritual   c. brogue
   b. ostracism   d. gospel   8. _____

9. ornate : showy :: pious : _____
   a. devout   **c.** paranoid
   b. prevalent   **d.** sacreligious   9. _____

10. incur : debt :: raze : _____
   a. repository   **c.** building
   b. brogue   **d.** lift up   10. _____

CONTEMPORARY POETRY
Robert Hayden
Dudley Randall

Unit Nine

Text pages 652–656

Text page 661

An Open-Book Test

A. Understanding Ideas and Poetic Techniques

Write the letter of the best answer to each question. (7 points each)

1. The father in "Those Winter Sundays" expresses his love
   a. through gentle and affectionate words
   b. through unselfish acts of devotion
   c. through gifts of clothing
   d. through discipline and routine   1. _____

2. From the poem we can infer several things about the speaker's family,
   but we do *not* know
   a. that the father worked as a laborer
   b. that the speaker had more than one pair of shoes
   c. that the family quarreled
   d. whether the mother was alive   2. _____

3. Which of the following statements about "The Whipping" is *not*
   accurate?
   a. The poem is written in four-line stanzas.
   b. The poem makes use of end rhyme.
   c. The speaker identifies with the boy who is whipped.
   d. The poem uses metaphor but not simile.   3. _____

4. From details in "The Whipping," we can infer several things, but we do
   not know
   a. that the old woman is fat
   b. that the old woman has beaten the boy before
   c. what the boy has done
   d. that the old woman has suffered   4. _____

5. When the speaker recalls his own punishment as a child, he remembers
   all of the following *except*
   a. his struggle to get free
   b. why he was beaten
   c. the harsh words that frightened him
   d. the change in the other person's face   5. _____

6. In "Runagate Runagate," the dangers faced by fleeing slaves include all of the following *except*
   a. scorpions   **b.** hunters   **c.** hounds   **d.** a river   6. _____

7. The verbs in line 1 of the poem refer to
   a. a subscriber   **b.** Harriet Tubman   **c.** the runagate   **d.** patterollers   7. _____

8. In "Runagate Runagate," Harriet Tubman is referred to by each of the following names *except*
   a. the General   **b.** Moses   **c.** Stealer of Slaves   **d.** Susyanna   8. _____

9. "George" is a poem about
   a. a changing relationship   **c.** the effects of aging
   b. the dangers of a foundry   **d.** a boy's devotion to his father   9. _____

10. Which of the following pairs is *not* accurate?
    a. Line 5: visual imagery   **c.** Line 11: personification
    b. Line 7: internal rhyme   **d.** Line 16: simile   10. _____

B. Vocabulary

Each of the following italicized words appears in one of the poems. Choose the best synonym or definition for each italicized word. (6 points each)

11. The boy spoke *indifferently* to his father.
    a. disrespectfully   **b.** anxiously   **c.** without interest   **d.** with concern   11. _____

12. Despite his *writhing*, he couldn't get free.
    a. crying   **b.** complaints   **c.** bellowing   **d.** twisting   12. _____

13. After the whipping, the woman felt *purged*.
    a. sorry   **b.** humiliated   **c.** cleansed   **d.** tranquil   13. _____

14. Harriet Tubman understood the fugitive's *anguish*.
    a. desire   **b.** experience   **c.** struggle   **d.** agony   14. _____

15. The men dodged the *monstrous* blocks.
    a. enormous   **b.** clumsy   **c.** dangerous   **d.** heavy   15. _____

C. Essay

Write a brief essay on this topic.

Discuss the character of the speaker in any of the poems by Hayden and Randall. Refer to specific evidence in the poem to support your conclusions.

Gwendolyn Brooks
Derek Walcott
Mari Evans

Text pages 665–667

Text page 671

Text page 676

An Open-Book Test

A. Understanding Ideas and Poetic Techniques

Write the letter of the best answer to each question. (10 points each)

1. Which of the following statements about "the sonnet-ballad" is *not* true?
   a. The rhyme scheme is that of a Shakespearean sonnet.
   b. There are five different rhymes in the poem.
   c. The speaker is identified in line 10.
   d. The poet uses alliteration and assonance in line 12.

   1. _____

2. Which of the following statements about "The Bean Eaters" is correct?
   a. The rhyme scheme is the same in each stanza.
   b. Most of the imagery appeals to the sense of sight.
   c. The poem depends mainly on figurative language.
   d. The diction is elegant.

   2. _____

3. In "We Real Cool," the reader can infer that the Golden Shovel is
   a. a hangout for the speakers
   b. a local movie theater
   c. a clubhouse
   d. a disco

   3. _____

4. In the selection from *Omeros*, each of the following lines contains a figure of speech *except*
   a. line 3   **c.** line 24
   b. line 5   **d.** line 26

   4. _____

5. Which of the following pairs is *not* correct?
   a. Line 20: alliteration
   b. Line 26: repetition
   c. Line 28: simile
   d. Line 31: personification

   5. _____

6. Which lines in "If There Be Sorrow" rhyme?
   a. Lines 3 and 7
   b. Lines 3 and 7; lines 6 and 9
   c. Lines 3 and 7; lines 4 and 8; lines 6 and 9
   d. Lines 3, 7, and 9

   6. _____

7. The lines that best explain the title of "The Rebel" are
   a. lines 3–5   c. lines 12–14
   b. lines 6–11   d. lines 1–2 and 6–10   7. _____

B. Vocabulary

Each of the following questions contains an italicized word that appears in one of the poems. Choose the best synonym or definition for each italicized word. (6 points each)

8. The meaning of the word *court* in line 10 of "the sonnet-ballad" is
   a. a courtyard   c. a formal gathering
   b. woo   d. respect   8. _____

9. *Impudent* beauty would be best described as
   a. modest   b. strange   c. bold   d. possessive   9. _____

10. Withering *tubers* are
    a. parts of a plant
    b. leaves of a vegetable
    c. poisonous plants
    d. knobby swellings   10. _____

11. Splendor that is *epical* is
    a. visually spectacular
    b. noble and heroic
    c. of historical interest
    d. fictitious   11. _____

12. The *reverberation* of thunderclaps refers to
    a. reflected light   c. deafening noise
    b. musical sound   d. reechoed sound   12. _____

C. Essay

Write a brief essay on this topic. Refer to the poem as often as you wish.

Images may appeal to any of the five senses: sight, hearing, touch, taste, and smell. Sometimes a single image appeals to more than one sense. Choose any of the poems by Brooks and Walcott and analyze its imagery. Tell why the individual images are effective.

Amiri Baraka
Sonia Sanchez
Julia Fields

An Open-Book Test

A. Understanding Ideas and Poetic Techniques

Write the letter of the best answer to each question. (10 points each)

1. In "Preface to a Twenty Volume Suicide Note," the poet uses hyperbole,
   or exaggeration, in all of the following *except*
   a. the title   **c.** line 11
   b. line 10   **d.** line 15   1. _____

2. The diction in "Preface to a Twenty Volume Suicide Note" is best
   described as
   a. formal   **c.** slangy
   b. conversational   **d.** elegant   2. _____

3. Which of the following statements about "SOS" is accurate?
   a. The poem uses no punctuation.
   b. The poem uses end rhyme.
   c. The poem is a call for help.
   d. The poem has no rhythm.   3. _____

4. In "Graduation Notes," the major metaphor
   a. compares life to a journey
   b. compares one's birth to the sea
   c. compares growing up to fighting war
   d. compares adolescence to music   4. _____

5. In "Graduation Notes," the subject of the verb *Know* in line 18 is
   a. *I*, line 18
   b. *you*, line 19
   c. *heroes*, line 19
   d. *years*, line 19   5. _____

6. In the first seven lines of "High on the Hog," the poet uses all of the
   following techniques *except*
   a. alliteration   **c.** end rhyme
   b. personification   **d.** assonance   6. _____

7. In "High on the Hog," an example of personification occurs in
   a. line 21
   c. line 45
   b. line 22
   d. line 57

7. _____

8. The author refers to African American history in all of the following lines *except*
   a. lines 21–22
   c. lines 74–76
   b. lines 45–46
   d. lines 81–82

8. _____

B. Vocabulary

Choose the best synonym or definition for each italicized word. (5 points each)

9. A *preface* is best described as
   a. a preview
   b. an introductory statement
   c. an index to a book
   d. a summary

9. _____

10. A person described as *suave* would be
    a. well-mannered
    c. untrustworthy
    b. generous
    d. unfaithful

10. _____

11. When one pays *homage*, one
    a. bends the knee
    c. shows respect
    b. donates money
    d. clears a debt

11. _____

12. To *prime* tobacco is
    a. to cultivate it
    c. to use it
    b. to sell it
    d. to prepare it for market

12. _____

C. Essay

Write a brief essay on this topic. Refer to the poems as often as you wish.

The tone of a poem reveals the poet's attitude toward the material and the reader. Choose one or more of the poems by Baraka, Sanchez, and Fields, and discuss the tone of the work or works. Indicate how the tone is created through such elements as diction, imagery, figures of speech, exaggeration, irony, and the like.

Ishmael Reed
Al Young
Alice Walker

Text pages 697–699

Text page 703

Text page 707

An Open-Book Test

A. Understanding Ideas and Poetic Techniques

Write the letter of the best answer to each question. (10 points each)

1. The speaker in ".05"
   a. would like to wear a derby
   b. considers money more important than love
   c. has not been successful with women
   d. wants to fly to India

   1. _____

2. Which of the following statements is *not* an accurate description of "Beware: Do Not Read This Poem"?
   a. The poem uses unusual spellings.
   b. The poem uses only standard English.
   c. The poem is identified with the reader.
   d. The poem is identified with a mirror.

   2. _____

3. The device that dominates "Beware: Do Not Read This Poem" is that of
   a. rhyme   c. personification
   b. alliteration   d. simile

   3. _____

4. Reed uses parallelism in all of the following lines *except*
   a. lines 1–4   c. lines 21–26
   b. lines 16–18   d. lines 37–40

   4. _____

5. By the word *underground* in line 2 of "For Poets," the author probably means
   a. working in secrecy
   b. experimental or radical in point of view
   c. out of touch with nature
   d. hiding as a fugitive

   5. _____

6. Which of the following pairs is *not* an accurate description of "For Poets"?
   a. Line 2: assonance
   b. Lines 4–6: parallelism
   c. Lines 13–14: rhyme
   d. Line 17: personification

   6. _____

7. The diction in "For Poets" is best described as
   a. concrete
   b. abstract
   c. formal
   d. elegant

   7. _____

8. The background for the poem "Women" is
   a. the Civil Rights struggle for equal education
   b. the movement for women's rights
   c. the Montgomery Bus Boycott
   d. the March on Washington for Jobs and Freedom

   8. _____

9. The characteristic Walker emphasizes in "Women" is
   a. physical energy
   b. determination
   c. religious faith
   d. violence

   9. _____

10. The central metaphor of "Women" is developed in all of the following
    lines *except*
    a. lines 3–4
    b. lines 5–8
    c. lines 12–18
    d. lines 22–26

    10. _____

B. Essay

Write a brief essay on this topic. Refer to the poems as often as you wish.

As you have seen, contemporary poets often take liberties with
conventional rules of form and style. They may omit punctuation; they
may change natural word order; they may invent words or deliberately
misspell them. Discuss poetic license in any of the works by Reed,
Young, and Walker.

Ntozake Shange
Safiya Henderson
Rita Dove

Text page 711
Text page 714
Text page 719

An Open-Book Test

A. Understanding Ideas and Poetic Techniques

Write the letter of the best answer to each question. (10 points each)

1. In "senses of heritage," the subjects discussed by the poet's family included all of the following *except*
   a. politics   **c.** the arts
   b. ecology   **d.** religion

   1. _____

2. Line 10 of "senses of heritage" suggests that
   a. the family was concerned with social position
   b. the family members did not care for trees
   c. there were no trees on the family's property
   d. the family could not afford to have a garden

   2. _____

3. The poem "senses of heritage" draws a contrast between
   a. the country and the city
   b. talkative and untalkative people
   c. the past and the future
   d. different concepts of heritage

   3. _____

4. Which of the following statements about "harlem / soweto" is *not* accurate?
   a. The poem uses no internal punctuation.
   b. Proper nouns are not capitalized.
   c. The poem is written as free verse.
   d. The poem uses no rhyme.

   4. _____

5. The theme of "harlem / soweto" might be expressed as
   a. the international struggle for civil rights
   b. the parallels between ghettos and black townships
   c. the unity of Africans and African Americans
   d. the oppression of minorities

   5. _____

6. "Sisters" tells about
   a. the affection between two sisters
   b. the hardships of growing up
   c. the changing perceptions of an older sister
   d. the jealousy of an older child for a younger one   6. _____

7. The speaker called her sister various names, including all of the
   following *except*
   a. Bird of the Dead   c. Buzzard
   b. a snap-eyed imp   d. Schmawk Schmawk Bird   7. _____

8. The speaker's punishment is referred to in all of the following lines
   except
   a. line 10   c. line 15
   b. line 12   d. line 16   8. _____

9. Which of the following descriptions of "Sister" is *not* accurate?
   a. All the stanzas contain the same number of lines.
   b. The poem uses both alliteration and assonance.
   c. The poem uses metaphor but not simile.
   d. The poem uses no rhyme.   9. _____

10. Which of the following pairs in "Sisters" is *not* correct?"
    a. Lines 3–5: imagery
    b. Lines 7–8: metaphor
    c. Line 14: alliteration
    d. Lines 17–18: simile   10. _____

B. Essay

Write a brief essay on this topic. Refer to the poems as often as you wish

Several poems in this unit refer to family relationships. Choose any two
poems you have read and discuss the theme of the family as it is treated
in the poems.

Analogy Test 8

Recognizing Relationships in Verbal Analogies

Write the letter of the best answer to each question. (10 points each)

1. chronic : worry :: austere : _____
   a. complaint   **c.** surroundings
   b. indifference   **d.** severe   1. _____

2. vise : device : savanna : _____
   a. plain   **c.** vegetation
   b. workbench   **d.** lever   2. _____

3. incontinent : restrained :: impudent : _____
   a. impertinent   **c.** courteous
   b. uncontrolled   **d.** possessive   3. _____

4. prophetic : prophecy :: mythic : _____
   a. mythology   **c.** mythicize
   b. mythical   **d.** myth   4. _____

5. beckon : attract :: purge : _____
   a. call   **b.** cleanse   **c.** corrupt   **d.** lure   5. _____

6. taut : smile :: epical : _____
   a. classical   **c.** laughter
   b. events   **d.** tension   6. _____

7. hiding : thrashing : shackle : _____
   a. fastening   **c.** imprison
   b. beating   **d.** concealment   7. _____

8. anguish : joy : senile : _____
   a. confused   **c.** childlike
   b. happy   **d.** alert   8. _____

9. frantic : frantically :: monstrous : _____
   a. monstrously   **c.** monstrosity
   b. monster   **d.** monstrousness   9. _____

10. reclaim : recover :: churn : _____
   a. butter   **c.** cream
   b. shake   **d.** container   10. _____

CONTEMPORARY DRAMA
Introduction

Unit Ten

Text page 727

Understanding Main Ideas

Write the letter of the best answer to each question. (10 points each)

1. All of the following were well-known African American actors *except*
   a. James Hewlett
   b. William Wells Brown
   c. Ira Aldridge
   d. Charles Gilpin

   1. _____

2. The major objection to minstrel shows was that
   a. white performers took roles as blacks
   b. they imitated slave entertainments
   c. they were demeaning and offensive to blacks
   d. they used stale formulas

   2. _____

3. During the early decades of the twentieth century, the NAACP promoted the rise of serious drama in several ways, but *not* by
   a. providing a school for black actors
   b. publishing plays in the *Crisis*
   c. sponsoring an annual contest for playwrights
   d. helping to open black theaters

   3. _____

4. Which of the following was *not* an aim of the Federal Theater Project?
   a. To compete with major commercial theaters
   b. To provide work for unemployed theater people
   c. To bring serious drama to a large audience
   d. To end discrimination in the theater

   4. _____

5. The most successful black theater unit of the 1930s was
   a. the Pekin Players
   b. the Lincoln Theatre Troupe
   c. the Krigwa Players
   d. the Lafayette Theater

   5. _____

6. The first successful play by an African American was
   a. a story of black and white dock workers
   b. an adaptation of a Shakespearean tragedy
   c. a drama that denounced lynching
   d. a work about poverty and unemployment

   6. _____

7. Which of the following pairs is *not* correctly identified?
   a. Eulalie Spence: *The Fool's Errand*
   b. Rudolph Fisher: *Conjur Man Dies*
   c. Rose McClendon: *Big White Fog*
   d. Langston Hughes: *Don't You Want to Be Free?*

   7. _____

8. Which of the following statements about *A Raisin in the Sun* is *not* accurate?
   a. The play was commercially successful.
   b. It was the first play written by an African American woman.
   c. The play won the New York Drama Critics Circle Award.
   d. The play deals with a black ghetto family.

   8. _____

9. A leading figure in the Black Arts Movement of the sixties was
   a. Amiri Baraka   c. Lorraine Hansberry
   b. Ossie Davis   d. William Branch

   9. _____

10. Which of the following pairs is *not* correctly identified?
    a. James Baldwin: *Blues for Mr. Charlie*
    b. Ntozake Shange: *No Place to Be Somebody*
    c. Lonne Elder: *Ceremonies in Dark Old Men*
    d. Charles Fuller: *A Soldier's Play*

    10. _____

August Wilson
from The Piano Lesson

Text page 738

A. Understanding Main Ideas

Write the letter of the best answer to each question. (7 points each)

1. Which of these characters is *not* identified correctly?
   a. Avery Brown: an elevator operator
   b. Wining Boy: a musician and gambler
   c. Doaker Charles: Maretha's uncle
   d. Lymon Jackson: Boy Willie's partner   1. _____

2. The Yellow Dog is
   a. a saloon in Mississippi   c. a prison farm
   b. a name for a railroad   d. the name of Lymon's truck 2. _____

3. Boy Willie's rival for Sutter's land is
   a. Joel Nolander   c. Ed Saunders
   b. Robert Smith   d. Jim Stovall   3. _____

4. Who put the carvings on the piano?
   a. Robert Sutter   c. Mama Esther
   b. Boy Charles   d. Willie Boy   4. _____

5. How did Sutter lose his piano?
   a. Doaker and Wining Boy stole it.
   b. He traded it for some land.
   c. He sold it to Mama Ola.
   d. Boy Charles removed it on a wagon.   5. _____

6. How did Crawley die?
   a. He was pushed down a well.
   b. He was killed during a shootout.
   c. Boy Willie killed him by accident.
   d. He died of jaundice.   6. _____

7. Why is Berniece unwilling to sell the piano?
   a. She wants Maretha to become a piano teacher.
   b. The piano represents the history of her family.
   c. She hasn't been offered enough money.
   d. She believes her brother will try to cheat her.   7. _____

8. Doaker works
  a. in a pawnshop
  b. as a train conductor
  c. as a railroad cook
  d. in a restaurant

8. _____

9. Which of the following characters does *not* see Sutter's ghost?
  a. Avery   **b.** Berniece   **c.** Doaker   **d.** Maretha

9. _____

10. How is the conflict resolved?
  a. Boy Willie and Lymon go back home.
  b. Avery blesses the piano.
  c. Boy Willie overcomes Sutter's ghost.
  d. Berniece exorcizes Sutter's ghost by playing the piano.

10. _____

B. Vocabulary

Choose the best synonym or definition for each italicized word. (6 points each)

11. A *sparsely* furnished house
  a. contains little furniture
  b. has a cluttered appearance
  c. is attractive and stylish
  d. is filled with expensive belongings

11. _____

12. A *brash* manner is
  a. winsome   **b.** tactless   **c.** gentle   **d.** shy

12. _____

13. They sang the song with great *fervor*.
  a. amusement   **b.** accuracy   **c.** intensity of feeling   **d.** harmony

13. _____

14. Maretha let out a scream of *stark* terror.
  a. unbelievable   **b.** complete   **c.** familiar   **d.** numbing

14. _____

15. Avery tries to cleanse the humble *abode*.
  a. musical instrument
  b. haunted house
  c. furnishings
  d. dwelling place

15. _____

C. Essay

Write a brief essay on this topic. Refer to the play as often as you wish.

Consider the title of Wilson's play. Why do you think he called it *The Piano Lesson*? What is the "lesson" that the piano provides? What do the characters in the play learn? Cite specific evidence in the play in discussing your interpretation.

CONTEMPORARY AFRICAN LITERATURE   Unit Eleven
Introduction

Understanding Main Ideas
Write the letter of the best answer to each question. (10 points each)

1. The major conflict faced by modern Africans is
   a. how to change Western misconceptions of African cultures
   b. how to convince Africans to give up tribal loyalties
   c. how to reconcile traditional African practices and Western institutions
   d. how to pay for health care and technological inventions   1. _____

2. Which of the following statements about African literature is *not* accurate?
   a. Contemporary literature exists in many languages.
   b. All contemporary writers now compose in native African languages.
   c. There are two major categories of contemporary literature.
   d. During the colonial period, literature was written in European languages.   2. _____

3. Which of the following displaced Africans is *not* identified correctly?
   a. Francis Williams: a poet from Jamaica
   b. Abrasu Hannibal: a slave educated at the Russian court
   c. Phillis Wheatley: a Brazilian poet
   d. Jupiter Hammon: a lyric poet from Long Island   3. _____

4. During the nineteenth century, all the following works were translated into West African languages *except*
   a. *Gulliver's Travels*   c. hymnbooks
   b. the Bible   d. *Pilgrim's Progress*   4. _____

5. Which of the following statements is *not* an accurate description of early writing in African languages?
   a. These works attack African tribal cultures as pagan and satanic.
   b. These works reflect the beliefs and teachings of Christian missionaries.
   c. These works are highly influenced by African oral literature.
   d. This early literature is moralistic.   5. _____

6. Which of the following statements about Kwasi Fiawoo is *not* accurate?
   a. He was a West African writer.
   b. He was educated in the United States.
   c. He wrote a play that is a classic of Ewe literature.
   d. He denounced African culture.   6. _____

7. Important figures associated with the Négritude movement include all of the following *except*
   a. Wole Soyinka, of Nigeria
   b. Aimé Césaire, of Martinique
   c. Léopold Sédar Senghor, of Senegal
   d. Léon Damas, of Guyane   7. _____

8. Africans and West Indians living in Paris during the 1930s were attracted to African American literature for several reasons, but *not* because
   a. it dealt with themes related to black life
   b. it expressed no interest in Africa
   c. it reflected African American speech and music
   d. it celebrated the beauty of black women   8. _____

9. The central themes in contemporary African literature include all of the following *except*
   a. the reclaiming of African ancestry
   b. the interdependence between human beings and nature
   c. the romanticizing of colonization
   d. the economic and psychological effects of racism   9. _____

10. Black African women writers are particularly concerned with
   a. themes of a glorious African past
   b. the plight of Africans living abroad
   c. the problems of racism
   d. changing roles and relationships of African men and women   10. _____

Léopold Sédar Senghor
Be Not Amazed

Text page 811

Birago Diop
Souffles

Text page 815

An Open-Book Test

Understanding Ideas and Poetic Techniques

Write the letter of the best answer to each question. (10 points each)

1. In "Be Not Amazed," Senghor refers to several musical instruments, but
    not to
    a. a reed   **c.** a guitar
    b. a harp   **d.** a drum   1. _____

2. The speaker in "Be Not Amazed"
    a. is eager for the coming battle
    b. is certain that he will die in battle
    c. imagines his lover's reaction to his death
    d. cautions his beloved not to mourn his death   2. _____

3. The references to war in "Be Not Amazed" appeal chiefly to the sense of
    a. hearing   **b.** sight   **c.** touch   **d.** smell   3. _____

4. The word *purple* in line 5 suggests
    a. a color blending red and blue
    b. an emblem of royalty
    c. a discoloration
    d. brilliant or elaborate language   4. _____

5. *Lamenting* in line 8 of "Be Not Amazed" refers to
    a. *earth*, line 7
    b. *I*, line 7
    c. *beloved*, line 7
    d. *rhythm*, line 6   5. _____

6. In "Souffles," the poet achieves unity through all of the following devices *except*
   a. repetition of ideas
   b. uniform stanza length
   c. parallelism
   d. refrains

   6. _____

7. The "voices" in "Souffles" include all of the following *except*
   a. fire   b. water   c. wind   d. sand

   7. _____

8. The sounds in "Souffles" include all of the following *except*
   a. laughing   c. groaning
   b. weeping   d. murmuring

   8. _____

9. Which of the following statements about "Souffles" is correct?
   a. The ancestor spirits can be both seen and heard.
   b. The ancestor spirits are joyful.
   c. The ancestor spirits can be heard but not seen.
   d. The ancestor spirits exist only in nonliving things.

   9. _____

10. Each of the following lines is repeated in "Souffles" *except*
    a. line 1   c. line 15
    b. line 7   d. line 20

    10. _____

Camara Laye
from **The Dark Child**

Text page 823

A. Understanding Main Ideas

Write the letter of the best answer to each question. (10 points each)

1. Which of the following statement is *not* true?
   a. The society of the uninitiated is made up solely of boys.
   b. A crowd follows the tom-tom player.
   c. The elders are called big *Kondéns*.
   d. The ceremony is held after the feast of Ramadan.

   1. _____

2. The narrator's father advises him to
   a. join in the chanting and singing
   b. play his *coro* enthusiastically
   c. conceal his fear
   d. do whatever he is told by the elders

   2. _____

3. The initiation takes place
   a. in a secret place in pitch blackness
   b. in a hollow in the bush
   c. in a lion's lair beyond the village
   d. at sundown in a remote part of the concession

   3. _____

4. The boys are comforted by
   a. a huge wood fire
   b. the silence of their march
   c. the moonlight
   d. the departure of the grown men

   4. _____

5. The boys are startled when
   a. they hear the roaring of many lions
   b. they are told to assemble beneath the bombax tree
   c. they are made to kneel and hide their eyes
   d. they are told to get up

   5. _____

6. The instruction the boys receive consists of learning
   a. tribal history
   b. how to roar like lions
   c. to play a musical instrument
   d. words and tunes

   6. _____

B. Vocabulary

Choose the best synonym or definition for each italicized word. (10 points each)

7. The narrator was thinking about the *sumptuous* feast.
   a. important   c. lavish
   b. special   d. holiday   7. _____

8. Despite the *vigilance* of the elders, the boys were afraid.
   a. kindness   c. sympathy
   b. watchfulness   d. closeness   8. _____

9. No one had the *audacity* to disobey the elders.
   a. boldness   c. foolishness
   b. strength   d. cleverness   9. _____

10. The narrator *implored* Kondén Diara to return to the bush.
    a. told   c. informed
    b. asked   d. begged   10. _____

C. Essay

Choose one of the following topics for a brief essay. Refer to the selection as often as you like.

1. Describe the stages of the ceremony, beginning with the gathering together of the boys and ending with their initiation.

2. The religious ceremonies and customs of a people often reveal their most cherished values. To judge from the ceremony described in this selection, what conclusions can you draw about the values of the narrator's community? What qualities are emphasized in the education of young people?

James Matthews
The Park

Text page 834

A. Understanding Main Ideas

Write the letter of the best answer to each question. (10 points each)

1. At the opening of the story, the children in the park are doing all of the following *except*
   a. sliding down the chute
   b. using the swings
   c. playing hide-and-seek
   d. riding the merry-go-round

   1. _____

2. At the opening of the story, the boy
   a. is on his way to pick up laundry
   b. is delivering a bundle of clean clothing
   c. throws a lump of clay at boys in the park
   d. rides the merry-go-round at a fair ground

   2. _____

3. When he is in the white woman's kitchen, the boy feels
   a. curious   c. ill at ease
   b. angry   d. relieved

   3. _____

4. When the boy passes the park on his way home, he
   a. reads the notice board
   b. kicks a ball into the street
   c. runs by to avoid being seen by the attendant
   d. throws a bag of rubbish over the railings

   4. _____

5. The boy bursts into tears because
   a. his mother has scolded him
   b. the children won't let him play with the tires
   c. he is furious about being shut out of the park
   d. he is still hungry

   5. _____

6. The boy's chores at home include all of the following *except*
   a. shopping for food   c. washing the dishes
   b. clearing the table   d. carrying out the garbage

   6. _____

7. At night the boy gets into the park
   a. by slipping through the railings
   b. by climbing over the railings
   c. after breaking the lock on the gate
   d. by slipping under the bars   7. _____

B. Vocabulary

Choose the best synonym or definition for each italicized word. (6 points each)

8. The boy's voice was *audible.*
   a. trembling   c. capable of being heard
   b. furious   d. apologetic   8. _____

9. The boy watched the children *cavorting* on the grass.
   a. kicking one another   c. shrieking
   b. jumping playfully   d. running wildly   9. _____

10. He remained *oblivious* of his surroundings.
    a. unmindful   b. aware   c. ashamed   d. weary   10. _____

11. The mother's whine changed to *reproach.*
    a. fear   b. misery   c. melancholy   d. blame   11. _____

12. The boy was struck by the *magnitude* of an idea.
    a. greatness   b. danger   c. impulsiveness   d. excitement   12. _____

C. Essay

Write a brief essay on this topic.

Matthews does not identify any characters in the story by name. What do you think is the author's purpose in keeping the characters anonymous? Is this an effective way to express the universality of his theme? Refer to specific evidence in the story to support your interpretation.

Chinua Achebe
Dead Men's Path

Text page 847

A. Understanding Main Ideas

Write the letter of the best answer to each question. (10 points each)

1. Which of the following statements is *not* an accurate description of
   Michael Obi?
   a. He is young and energetic.
   b. His ideas about education are progressive.
   c. He encourages his colleagues to marry.
   d. He is an outspoken critic of other headmasters.   1. _____

2. Nancy's chief responsibility at the school is
   a. serving as the chairperson for committees
   b. tending the school gardens
   c. ordering furniture
   d. running the library   2. _____

3. According to the villagers, the footpath referred to in the title serves
   several functions. Which of the following is *not* one of them?
   a. It leads from the village shrine to the place of burial.
   b. It is the path used by ancestors.
   c. It is used by unborn children.
   d. The path is sacred to the earth goddess.   3. _____

4. Why are the schoolmaster's improvements ruined?
   a. The construction is against regulations.
   b. The villagers need a shortcut.
   c. The villagers wish to pacify the ancestors who have been insulted.
   d. The use of barbed wire is prohibited.   4. _____

5. Obi's attitude toward the villagers' beliefs might be described by all of
   the following words *except*
   a. objective   **c.** scornful
   b. arrogant   **d.** belittling   5. _____

B. Vocabulary

Choose the best synonym or definition for each of the following italicized words. (10 points each)

6. Michael Obi is considered *pivotal* in his profession.
   - **a.** trustworthy
   - **b.** essential
   - **c.** energetic
   - **d.** outspoken

   6. _____

7. His wife is accustomed to his *denigration* of certain ideas.
   - **a.** employment
   - **b.** acceptance
   - **c.** belittling
   - **d.** questioning

   7. _____

8. The carefully cultivated school gardens contrast with the *rank* neighborhood bushes.
   - **a.** ugly
   - **b.** overgrown
   - **c.** offensive
   - **d.** thorny

   8. _____

9. Obi wishes to *eradicate* pagan rituals.
   - **a.** wipe out
   - **b.** outlaw
   - **c.** examine
   - **d.** replace

   9. _____

10. Obi is criticized for his misguided *zeal*.
    - **a.** philosophy
    - **b.** action
    - **c.** passion
    - **d.** reform

    10. _____

C. Essay

Write a brief essay on the following topic.

The introduction to this unit states: "Nigerian and black South African writers are . . . concerned with demonstrating how difficult it is to reconstruct a precolonial African culture free of Westernization." Discuss how this theme is treated in "Dead Men's Path." Refer to the selection as often as you wish.

Wole Soyinka
from **Aké**   Text page 854
Telephone Conversation   Text page 869

A. Understanding Main Ideas

Write the letter of the best answer to each question. (7 points each)

1. At the school in Aké, Wole observes all of the following *except*
   a. children marching into school, singing songs
   b. poor students being disciplined
   c. children taking care of the school grounds
   d. school uniforms   1. _____

2. When Wole follows his sister to the infant school,
   a. the teachers become flustered
   b. his name is entered in the register
   c. his sister refuses to talk to him
   d. he becomes quickly bored and returns home   2. _____

3. Wole is late getting to lunch because
   a. he and Mr. Olagbaju are playing *ayo*
   b. the teachers make a fuss over him
   c. he is fascinated by objects in the empty schoolroom
   d. he doesn't like pounded yam   3. _____

4. After he is injured at the Canon's residence, Wole
   a. worries about the blood he has lost
   b. wants to get even with Osiki
   c. never gets back on a see-saw
   d. insists on having his *dansiki* washed   4. _____

5. Missing from Wole's account of his birthday party is any mention of
   a. foods   b. games   c. entertainment   d. gifts   5. _____

6. According to Wole, the *egúngún* are
   a. professional musicians   c. acrobats
   b. spirits of the dead   d. kidnappers   6. _____

7. Wole is injured again
   a. while playing with a cutlass
   b. during an *egúngún* procession
   c. while running from Osiki
   d. during a fight between two older students   7. _____

8. The speaker in "Telephone Conversation"
   a. wants to be interviewed for a job
   b. is looking for a roommate
   c. is trying to locate an office
   d. wishes to rent a place to live   8. _____

9. The speaker admits that he is African because
   a. he is required to do so
   b. he doesn't wish to waste his time
   c. he doesn't like the woman's tone
   d. he believes he can get a lower price   9. _____

10. We can assume that the speaker
   a. is not familiar with the English language
   b. enjoys humiliating people
   c. has a sense of humor
   d. sympathizes with the woman's position   10. _____

B. Vocabulary

Choose the best synonym for each italicized word. (6 points each)

11. The teachers had an *indulgent* smile on their faces.
   a. easy-going   **b.** uneasy   **c.** animated   **d.** overeager   11. _____

12. Wole followed his sister at a *discreet* distance.
   a. great   **b.** distinct   **c.** careful   **d.** marked   12. _____

13. Wole became the teacher's *accomplice*.
   a. favorite pupil   **c.** close friend
   b. partner in crime   **d.** trusted monitor   13. _____

14. Wole tried to *emulate* Osiki's pace
   a. follow   **b.** catch up with   **c.** slow down   **d.** imitate   14. _____

15. He thought the location of the rooms *indifferent*.
   a. ideal   **b.** important   **c.** insignificant   **d.** problematic   15. _____

C. Essay

Write a brief essay on the following topic.

What impression do you have of Soyinka's childhood from the excerpt
in your textbook? Consider his memories of school, of his family and
friends, and of his own perceptions of events. Can you find evidence of
imagination and keen powers of observation in Soyinka as a small child?

Ngugi wa Thiong'o
The Return

Text page 873

A. Understanding Main Ideas

Write the letter of the best answer to each question. (10 points each)

1. The main character in the story is returning from
   a. warfare   **c.** a local jail
   b. exile abroad   **d.** a detention camp

   1. _____

2. How does the landscape change as Kamau approaches his village?
   a. The roads become dry and dusty.
   b. Trees and green bush appear.
   c. The terrain becomes steep and rocky.
   d. The paths become muddy.

   2. _____

3. After he meets the group of village women, Kamau feels
   a. pleasantly excited
   b. relieved
   c. excluded from a secret
   d. triumphant

   3. _____

4. As he approaches the village, Kamau plans
   a. to build a new house
   b. to become a farmer
   c. to leave the country
   d. to pay his wife's bride price

   4. _____

5. When Kamau finds his father, the old man expresses
   a. fear   **b.** joy   **c.** bitterness   **d.** grief

   5. _____

6. His parents allowed Muthoni to leave because
   a. they could not take care of her
   b. Karanja offered them money
   c. she was impatient to go
   d. they were ashamed of her

   6. _____

B. Vocabulary

Choose the best synonym or definition for each italicized word. (10 points each)

7. Kamau felt a strong *nostalgia* for the past.
   a. distaste
   b. bitterness
   c. longing
   d. exuberance

   7. _____

8. He vowed that no one would *flout* his manhood again.
   a. deny   b. abuse   c. scorn   d. harm

   8. _____

9. Disbelief was *discernible* in the old man's eyes.
   a. lacking
   b. recognizable
   c. vanishing
   d. persistent

   9. _____

10. Kamau wished to *denounce* everything.
    a. condemn   b. leave   c. destroy   d. forget

    10. _____

C. Essay

Write a brief essay on the following topic. Refer to the selection as often as you wish.

A short story, as you have seen, has both a foreground and a background. Discuss the background of "The Return"—the time and place of events and the circumstances affecting the characters. What do you learn about the effect of the Mau Mau conflict on village people?

Analogy Test 9

Recognizing Relationships in Verbal Analogies

Write the letter of the best answer to each question. (10 points each)

1. deity : worship :: injury : _____
   a. redress
   b. transgress
   c. reproach
   d. prescribe

   1. _____

2. sumptuous : feast :: pagan : _____
   a. revel
   b. tumultuous
   c. satanic
   d. qualm

   2. _____

3. audacity : boldness :: treachery : _____
   a. loyalty
   b. perfidy
   c. arrogance
   d. treason

   3. _____

4. rancid : odor :: haggard : _____
   a. smell
   b. foul
   c. features
   d. worn

   4. _____

5. implement : tool :: stigma : _____
   a. instrument
   b. stature
   c. disgrace
   d. phenomenon

   5. _____

6. commence : terminate :: resurrect : _____
   a. use
   b. hover
   c. complete
   d. bury

   6. _____

7. lair : lion :: shrine : _____
   a. den
   b. rite
   c. goddess
   d. pagan

   7. _____

8. thoroughfare : traffic :: peroxide : _____
   a. chemical
   b. blond
   c. route
   d. hair

   8. _____

9. affront : confront :: accede : _____
    a. concede   **c.** encounter
    b. offend   **d.** proceed   **9.** _____

10. impersonality : person :: unprogressive : _____
    a. progression   **c.** docile
    b. progress   **d.** progressive   **10.** _____

THE NOVEL
Buchi Emecheta
The Wrestling Match

Unit Twelve

Text page 893

Chapters 1–7

A. Understanding Main Ideas

Write the letter of the best answer to each question. (10 points each)

1. Okei survived the civil war because
   a. he was in another village when his parents were killed
   b. he went out into the back yard when the soldiers came
   c. his parents hid him before they were killed
   d. the soldiers spared his life   1. _____

2. The boys of Okei's age-group have been accused of
   a. insulting the villagers
   b. beating up young children
   c. stealing from old people
   d. selling palm-wine to strangers   2. _____

3. The purpose of the wrestling match is
   a. to teach the elders a lesson
   b. to choose a leader for the age-group
   c. to avoid working on the farms
   d. to settle a dispute with the villagers of Akpei   3. _____

4. Okei tells Kwutelu that
   a. he will get thieves to burgle her father's compound
   b. he is a champion wrestler
   c. she has been stealing fish from streams in Akpei
   d. he will never marry her   4. _____

5. Kwutelu decides to go to her father's sleeping-house
   a. because he is expecting her
   b. to avoid waking up her mother
   c. to discuss her bride-price with him
   d. because there are guests in her mother's hut   5. _____

B. Vocabulary

Choose the best synonym or definition for each italicized word or phrase.
(10 points each)

6. Obi Agiliga's meal was *disrupted*.
   a. served
   b. tasteless
   c. disturbed
   d. ruined

   6. _____

7. The civil war had *culminated in* the creation of a new nation.
   a. begun with
   b. forced
   c. prevented
   d. resulted in

   7. _____

8. *Insinuations* are
   a. direct accusations
   b. hints or suggestions
   c. indirect compliments
   d. mocking laughs

   8. _____

9. The farm hands *ambled* into the bush for shelter.
   a. hastened anxiously
   b. sprinted gracefully
   c. walked in a leisurely way
   d. scurried nervously

   9. _____

10. Okei considered Kwutelu *arrogant*.
    a. haughty   **b.** agile   **c.** talkative   **d.** silly

    10. _____

The Wrestling Match

Chapters 8–14

A. Understanding Main Ideas

Write the letter of the best answer to each question. (10 points each)

1. Uche's reaction to Kwutelu's accident is
   a. amusement   **c.** sympathy
   b. astonishment   **d.** anger   1. _____

2. The girls of Igbuno decide to sell their plantain in Akpei
   a. because there is no market in Igbuno
   b. in order to make more money
   c. so that they will avoid Okei and his friends
   d. because the Igbuno villagers have boycotted their wares   2. _____

3. Okei decides to consult his uncle for several reasons. Which of the
   following is *not* one of them?
   a. Okei respects the wisdom of the village elders.
   b. The Akpei boys are being helped by their elders.
   c. Okei and his age-mates do not know the wrestling dance.
   d. Okei's uncle was a good wrestler in his time.   3. _____

4. Okei's uncle teaches him all of the following *except*
   a. how to take his opponent unawares
   b. how to strengthen his legs through running
   c. how to give the audience pleasure
   d. the songs and style of the wrestling dance   4. _____

5. What is the outcome of the contest?
   a. Okei wins three wrestling matches.
   b. Nduka and Okei win all wrestling matches.
   c. Okei wins only the final match.
   d. Okei wins two out of three wrestling matches.   5. _____

B. Vocabulary

Choose the best synonym or definition for each italicized word. (10 points each)

6. Uche found the wrestling practice *rigorous*.
   a. stimulating
   b. pleasurable
   c. strenuous
   d. necessary

   6. _____

7. One girl had a *woebegone* look on her face.
   a. sly
   b. mocking
   c. mischievous
   d. miserable

   7. _____

8. Okei's *insolent* tone was disregarded.
   a. gentle
   b. grumbling
   c. rude
   d. anxious

   8. _____

9. Okei said that the girls' money would be *eroded*.
   a. used up
   b. stolen
   c. insufficient
   d. lost

   9. _____

10. The girls' *tunics* were admired.
    a. hairdos
    b. loose-fitting garments
    c. acrobatic feats
    d. symbolic cloaks

    10. _____

C. Essay

Write a brief essay on the following topic. Refer to the selection as often as you wish.

In a short story or novel, the main characters often experience some change, either in circumstances or in understanding. Which of the characters in *The Wrestling Match* undergo some significant change? Identify the characters and tell whether the change is external or internal.

Analogy Test 10

Recognizing Relationships in Verbal Analogies

Write the letter of the best answer to each question. (10 points each)

1. corrugated : sheets :: garnished : _____
   a. roofs   c. food
   b. metals   d. matches   1. _____

2. ransacked : burglar :: sprinted : _____
   a. pilferer   c. seller
   b. agile   d. runner   2. _____

3. abusive : abuse :: conspiratorial : _____
   a. conspiracy   c. conspire
   b. conspiring   d. conspirator   3. _____

4. compulsory : course :: cunning : _____
   a. trick   c. cheeky
   b. shrewdness   d. playful   4. _____

5. impenetrable : clear :: incredulous : _____
   a. evident   c. strange
   b. believing   d. penetration   5. _____

6. hefty : chest :: resonant : _____
   a. muscular   c. drum
   b. strength   d. pulsate   6. _____

7. profusely : abundantly :: reflectively : _____
   a. thoughtfully   c. carefully
   b. excessively   d. indulgently   7. _____

8. pungent : song :: derisive : _____
   a. insulting   c. biting
   b. smile   d. scornful   8. _____

9. gourd : water : : shell : _____
   a. fruit   **c.** skin
   b. hollow   **d.** toughness   **9.** _____

10. imperative : necessary : : compulsory : _____
   a. cunning   **c.** competent
   b. education   **d.** obligatory   **10.** _____

Review and Mastery Tests

Writing a Précis

A *précis* is a brief summary of another work. In writing a précis, you restate the principal ideas or events of that work in your own words. A précis is similar to a paraphrase.

Here are steps to follow in writing a précis:

1. Make sure you are familiar with the work you are condensing.

2. Choose only the most important details for inclusion. Do not leave out any essential facts.

3. Replace the author's words with your own language. If you use any of the author's phrases, enclose them in quotation marks.

4. Connect your ideas with transitional expressions.

5. If the précis is very short (100 words or less), use a single paragraph. Otherwise, group your ideas into two or more paragraphs.

6. In revising, look for ways to condense your précis further.

Assignment

Choose one of the selections in the unit and write a précis. Try not to exceed 300 words.

Analyzing Theme

The *theme* of a work is its central or dominant meaning. Theme usually involves some insight into life or human behavior. The theme of a work is not always obvious. Sometimes you need to think about a work carefully before you understand its theme. A theme can sometimes be expressed as a single sentence. Often, however, you need a paragraph or a complete essay to state the basic meaning of a literary work or group of works.

Here are steps to follow in writing about theme:

1. As you reread the work, look for direct statements of theme.

2. Locate any key words, passages, images, or symbols. Sometimes an author uses repetition to emphasize important ideas.

3. Get a general impression of the author's purpose and method. After you understand what happens in the story or the poem, ask yourself what larger meaning this experience may have.

4. Express the main idea of the selection in one or two sentences.

5. Test your thematic statement by applying it to important details in the selection. Does your statement take into account *all* important actions, symbols, images?

6. Develop your thematic statement into an essay by referring to specific evidence in the literature.

Assignment

Here are some of the recurrent ideas in African American literature. Choose one of these for development into an essay on theme. Then locate two or more selections in your textbook that illustrate some aspect of the theme. Formulate a statement of theme and show how this theme is treated in each of the selections.

Freedom Through Literacy

The Uses of the Past

The Dual Heritage of African Americans

The Oral Tradition in African American Literature

Analyzing Style

Style is the term used for the way someone writes. Style refers to the various qualities and characteristics that go into a piece of writing: words and expressions, sentence structure, imagery, rhythm, figurative language, and the like. Some writers' styles are so distinctive that they can be recognized even without the author's signature. Style is often a key to *tone*, the writer's attitude toward a subject, a character, or the reader.

Here are steps to follow in writing about style:

1. Read for a general impression of the work. Is the work serious or humorous? Is it formal or informal? Is the tone satirical or ironic?

2. Note the kinds of words used and the order of words in sentences. Does the author tend to use simple words in clear order? Are the sentences complex or lengthy? Is the choice of words and sentence structure appropriate for the author's subject?

3. Note the techniques used to develop ideas. Does the author use such devices as *allusion, parallelism, repetition*? If so, for what purpose?

4. Does the author have certain habits of organization, such as using comparison and contrast or cause and effect to develop ideas?

5. In descriptive passages, does the author depend on many adjectives or are descriptions scaled down? Does the author use dialogue to present characters or are they presented directly through description?

6. Write a sentence that sums up the major features of the writer's style.

Assignment

Choose a passage of prose from one of the selections in the unit and analyze its style. In your discussion include a statement that gives a general impression of the writer's style. Then support that statement with specific examples of the kinds of words used, the length of sentences, literary devices, and other characteristics.

Writing a Critique

A *critique* is a critical analysis of a literary work. A critique evaluates an entire work or some aspect of it in order to arrive at some judgment of the literary merit of the piece. In writing a critique, you attempt not only to understand what the writer has done, but also to determine if what has been done has been done effectively.

To judge a literary work, you need to set it against certain *criteria* or standards. In writing a critique of a short story or novel, for example, you would need to determine first the criteria for judging such elements as *plot, character, setting, point of view, tone,* and *theme.* In writing a critique of a poem, you would need to establish your criteria for judging such elements as *diction, imagery, figurative language,* and *rhyme* as well as criteria for structure and form.

Here are steps to follow in writing a critique:

1. Begin with a set of questions you will use to evaluate literary content and form. For a critique of poetry, you might develop questions along these lines:

   What form has the poet chosen (*sonnet, free verse,* etc.)? Is this form appropriate for the subject of the poem?

   Are there words in the poem with strong associations or connotations?

   Are the images and figures of speech well chosen? Are they imaginative?

   Are symbols and allusions clear? Are they effective?

   Are the sounds of the poem (*rhyme, alliteration, assonance,* etc.) related to its meaning?

   What is the purpose of the poem? Has the poet achieved that purpose?

2. Write a sentence that expresses the total effect of the work you are evaluating. This statement should become the thesis of your essay.

3. Support your judgment with evidence from the literary work.

Assignment

Choose one literary work or a group of literary works for evaluation. In your essay, be sure to include a statement giving your opinion. Then support your position by drawing on specific evidence in the selection or selections that demonstrates the validity of your position.

NAME _____ CLASS _____ DATE _____

Relating a Literary Work to Its Historical Period

A work of literature reflects the period in which it was composed and can reveal a great deal about the customs and values of a specific time and place. A literary work also reflects the traditions of its own time in terms of language and ideas. When you write about literature from the vantage point of its historical period, you try to cast light on its form and content.

Here are steps to follow in writing an essay on historical contexts:

1. Focus on a topic to be investigated or a problem to be solved. Phrase this as a question: "How does the work deal with the everyday life of slaves in the early nineteenth century?" "What were the effects of the Great Depression on the people in the rural South?"

2. In rereading the literary work, distinguish those details that relate to your subject.

3. Interpret the evidence and state your conclusion in a sentence that will serve as the thesis of your essay.

4. Develop your thesis statement with specific evidence from the literature.

Assignment

Choose one or more selections in which the writer gives a picture of life at a specific period of history. Briefly discuss the background of the selection and tell how the work deals with the issues or conditions of the period.

Practice in Reading Comprehension

Developing Reading Comprehension Skills

Standardized tests frequently ask you to read several passages and to analyze the structure and meaning of each one. Reading comprehension questions test your ability to understand ideas that are expressed directly and ideas that must be inferred from the material.

Read the following excerpt from the *Narrative of the Life of Frederick Douglass, an American Slave.* As you read, try to get a general impression of the main ideas, the author's attitude toward his material, and the way the author develops his ideas. Then go on to the questions. As you work on the questions, refer to the passage as often as you need to. When you have made your choices, check your answers in the Self-Check Answer Key.

> My mistress was, as I have said, a kind and tender-hearted woman; and in the simplicity of her soul she commenced, when I first went to live with her, to treat me as she supposed one human being ought to treat another. In entering upon the duties of a slaveholder, she did not seem to perceive that I sustained to her the relation of a mere chattel, and that for her to treat me as a human being was not only wrong, but dangerously so. Slavery proved as injurious to her as it did to me. When I went there, she was a pious, warm, and tender-hearted woman. There was no sorrow or suffering for which she had not a tear. She had bread for the hungry, clothes for the naked, and comfort for every mourner that came within her reach. Slavery soon proved its ability to divest her of these heavenly qualities. Under its influence, the tender heart became stone, and the lamblike disposition gave way to one of tiger-like fierceness. The first step in her downward course was in her ceasing to instruct me. She now commenced to practise her husband's precepts. She finally became even more violent in her opposition than her husband himself. She was not satisfied with simply doing as well as he had commanded; she seemed anxious to do better. Nothing seemed to make her more angry than to see me with a newspaper. She seemed to think that here lay the danger. I have had her rush at me with a face made all up of fury, and snatch from me a newspaper, in a manner that fully revealed her apprehension. She was an apt woman; and a little experience soon demonstrated, to her satisfaction, that education and slavery were incompatible with each other.

1. The main idea of this passage is that
    a. slaveholders are brutal
    b. the author is surprised at the change in his mistress's behavior
    c. slavery is destructive to the slaveholder as well as to the slave
    d. power corrupts people
    e. women slaveholders are more vicious than their male counterparts   1. _____

Hint: Look for a sentence that states the main idea. If there is a topic sentence in the paragraph, restate its meaning in your own words.

2. In this passage Douglass uses all of the following methods of development *except*
   a. chronology
   b. contrast
   c. cause and effect
   d. main idea and examples
   e. spatial order

2. _____

Hint: Test each choice against the passage and eliminate the wrong choice.

3. It can be inferred from this passage that
   a. no slaves were allowed to read
   b. slaveholders feared that learning to read would make slaves unmanageable
   c. slaveholders did not believe slaves had the ability to master reading
   d. the desire to read was unusual on the part of slaves
   e. most slaveholders approved only of slaves reading the Bible

3. _____

Hint: The inference must be drawn from the facts in the passage, not from other sources.

4. It can be inferred from this passage that Douglass
   a. expected his mistress to treat him with increasing harshness
   b. was too discouraged to continue his instruction
   c. defied his mistress openly
   d. did not need any help in learning to read
   e. hoped his mistress would have a change of heart

4. _____

Self-Check Answer Key
   1. c
   2. e
   3. b
   4. a

Developing Reading Comprehension Skills

Read the following excerpt from W. E. B. Du Bois's *The Souls of Black Folk*. Then go on to the questions. Refer to the passage as often as you need to. When you have made your choices, check your answers in the Self-Check Answer Key.

The greatest success of the Freedmen's Bureau lay in the planting of the free school among Negroes, and the idea of free elementary education among all classes in the South. It not only called the school-mistresses through the benevolent agencies and built them school-houses, but it helped discover and support such apostles of human culture as Edmund Ware, Samuel Armstrong and Erastus Cravath. The opposition to Negro education in the South was at first bitter, and showed itself in ashes, insult, and blood; for the South believed an educated Negro to be a dangerous Negro. And the South was not wholly wrong; for education among all kinds of men always has had, and always will have, an element of danger and revolution, of dissatisfaction and discontent. Nevertheless, men strive to know. Perhaps some inkling of this paradox, even in the unquiet days of the Bureau, helped the Bayonets allay an opposition to human training which still to-day lies smouldering in the South, but not flaming. Fisk, Atlanta, Howard, and Hampton were founded in these days, and six million dollars were expended for educational work, seven hundred and fifty thousand dollars of which the freedmen themselves gave of their poverty.

1. Which of these statements best expresses the main idea of the passage?
   a. The Freedmen's Bureau advanced the course of education in the South.
   b. The Freedmen's Bureau was unable to overcome opposition to free elementary education.
   c. The Freedmen's Bureau had limited funds for educational work.
   d. The concept of the free school was a radical idea.
   e. Without the Freedmen's Bureau, no schools would have been built for Negroes.   1. _____

Hint: Look for a sentence that states the main idea. Restate its meaning in your own words.

2. The events described in this passage occurred during
   a. the years before emancipation of the slaves
   b. the Reconstruction period following the American Civil War
   c. the period between World War I and World War II
   d. the decade of the Great Depression
   e. the post-World War II period   2. _____

Hint: What clues are provided by names and events?

3. From the passage, we can infer that Edmund Ware, Samuel Armstrong, and Erastus Cravath were
   a. millionaires who supported charities
   b. religious leaders
   c. teachers who promoted education in Southern schools
   d. politicians at the Freedmen's Bureau
   e. lawyers from the North

3. _____

Hint: Test each choice against the passage and eliminate the wrong choices.

4. We can assume that the author of this passage
   a. worked for the Freedmen's Bureau
   b. believes that education is dangerous
   c. sees a connection between education and desire for change
   d. taught at one of the free schools
   e. feels that opposition to the free schools was justified

4. _____

Hint: Avoid misinterpretation by rereading relevant details in the passage.

5. In referring to his own time, the author believes that opposition to Negro education in the South
   a. is gaining strength
   b. has been effectively outlawed
   c. can never be rooted out
   d. is an indirect result of the Freedmen's Bureau
   e. has subsided but still exists

5. _____

Hint: Examine the author's metaphor carefully.

Self-Check Answer Key
1. a
2. b
3. c
4. c
5. e

Developing Reading Comprehension Skills

The following excerpt from *Behind the Scenes*, by Elizabeth Keckley, deals with events in Washington, D.C., during 1865. After you have read the passage, answer the questions. Check your answers in the Self-Check Answer Key.

The days passed without any incident of particular note disturbing the current of life. On Friday morning, April 14th—alas! what American does not remember the day—I saw Mrs. Lincoln but for a moment. She told me that she was to attend the theatre that night with the President, but I was not summoned to assist her in making her toilette. Sherman had swept from the northern border of Georgia through the heart of the Confederacy down to the sea, striking the death-blow to the rebellion. Grant had pursued General Lee beyond Richmond, and the army of Virginia, that had much such stubborn resistance, was crumbling to pieces. Fort Sumter had fallen;—the stronghold first wrenched from the Union, and which had braved the fury of Federal guns for so many years, was restored to the Union; the end of the war was near at hand, and the great pulse of the loyal North thrilled with joy. The dark war-cloud was fading, and a white-robed angel seemed to hover in the sky, whispering "Peace—peace on earth, good-will toward men!" Sons, brothers, fathers, friends, sweethearts were coming home. Soon the white tents would be folded, the volunteer army be disbanded, and tranquillity again reign. Happy, happy day!—happy at least to those who fought under the banner of the Union. There was great rejoicing throughout the North. From the Atlantic to the Pacific, flags were gayly thrown to the breeze, and at night every city blazed with its tens of thousand lights. But scarcely had the fireworks ceased to play, and the lights been taken down from the windows, when the lightning flashed the most appalling news over the magnetic wires. "The President has been murdered!" spoke the swift-winged messenger, and the loud huzza died upon the lips. A nation suddenly paused in the midst of festivity, and stood paralyzed with horror—transfixed with awe.

1. We can assume from details in this passage that the narrator
   a. was a close personal friend of the Lincoln family
   b. lived in the White House
   c. worked for Mrs. Lincoln
   d. was a visitor to the capital
   e. was a governess in the Lincoln household

1. _____

Hint: Locate the sentences that pinpoint the answer for you.

2. The sentences in this passage are arranged for the purpose of stressing
   a. chronological order
   b. spatial order
   c. details and examples
   d. cause-and-effect relationships
   e. contrast in moods

   2. _____

Hint: Test each choice against the structure of the passage and eliminate the wrong choices.

3. Which of these might be an appropriate title for the passage?
   a. War and Peace
   b. The End of an Era
   c. The Death of a President
   d. Triumph and Tragedy
   e. The Paths of Glory

   3. _____

Hint: Consider the entire passage in making your choice.

4. According to this passage, the news of Lincoln's assassination was spread by
   a. lightning
   b. telephone
   c. messengers
   d. telegraph
   e. word of mouth

   4. _____

Hint: Look for a phrase that describes the medium of communication.

5. The "loud huzza" refers to
   a. shouts of joy
   b. exploding fireworks
   c. noisemakers
   d. patriotic songs
   e. military music

   5. _____

Hint: Examine the context in which the word *huzza* appears to infer its meaning.

Self-Check Answer Key
   1. c
   2. e
   3. d
   4. d
   5. a

Sharpening Your Test-Taking Skills in Reading and Writing

Responding to Reading-Assessment Questions

A. Reading a Group of Selections Related by Theme

Read the selections that follow and answer the multiple-choice questions. As you read, keep in mind the theme and focus question.

Theme

Family members and traditions help shape who we are and help us grow as people.

Focus Question

Why is it important for traditions and values to be passed down from one generation to another?

Family Fabrics (Magazine Article)
Atiya Butler

I have very few memories of my great-grandmother. The ones I do possess are dreamy recollections of a woman we visited one summer in Alabama when I was four or five. In the strongest of these I see her fanning me as I complain incessantly about the heat. But when I try to focus on her face, I draw a blank.

My childhood memories of New York in early February are far more vivid. Though there were numerous blankets and comforters to keep me warm when ice frosted my bedroom window, my mother would place an extra, heavier blanket at the foot of my bed. It was unusual, with pink and gray cloth patches and assorted strings sticking out of the corners, middle, and sides. When no one was looking, I would pull the strings tighter and form double knots in the center of each piece of worn fabric. Wrapping it around me in the middle of the night, my mother would quietly tell me that the blanket was unlike anything else we had: It was a "quilt." And she would smile in an odd way as she remembered the woman who had made it— her grandmother Aggie—the outlines of whose face slowly slipped away from me year by year.

My great-grandmother quilted for most of her adult life. She often used scraps of old dress material and multicolored strings as the basis for her designs. Either by joining squares or strips of fabric (a method known as piecing) or by sewing material cut into various designs directly onto quilt tops (known as appliqué) she made numerous bedcovers for her husband and eight children. Old cotton sheets or discarded flour sacks, some indelibly etched with the blue imprint of company labels, provided the backings. As the years advanced and her skills as a seamstress improved, her quilts became more detailed, the arrangement of materials and stitching more precise. Before she died in 1984, she tried to ensure that the family would never be without quilts; each of her daughters as well as every one of her granddaughters received at least one.

Within my immediate circle of relatives, we own seven. But for me our quilts are much more than family mementos. They are crucial memory joggers. One of my aunt's quilts, for example, is made up of dresses she wore while skipping rope in Harlem during the early 1950s. The checkerboard and striped print outfits my grandmother sent to Birmingham as hand-me-downs were eventually cut into long strips, sewn together, and placed in an erratic pattern against an orange and white backing. Another example (which my grandmother keeps folded under her mattress) is affectionately known as the britches quilt, because it is made out of the trousers of various uncles, brothers, and sons, shaped into squares and tied with red strings in the center of each patch. When my grandmother (Great-Grandma Aggie's oldest child and the person with the firmest grasp on our family history) looks at one of our quilts, she amazingly remembers what pieces came from where. She will gladly tell you about quilting parties and quiet moments spent watching women of widely varying ages and abilities create what to them were simple household items but to the modern observer are clearly works of art.

For many black families with strong ties to rural Southern communities, quilts represent part of a tradition of craftsmanship that stretches back hundreds of years. African-American quilts pass from generation to generation, with knowledge of the quilts' origins and whereabouts rarely being shared with outsiders. Like most quilters, my great-grandmother had a keen eye for color and pattern, but she probably didn't suspect that she was making art. Yet over the years, as quilts became separated from the people who made and owned them, often ending up in antiques shops and museums, they have taken on a new celebrity, and with a spate of exhibits, conferences, and books, experts are seeking to follow the lost strands of quilt history. As part of this effort, African-American quilts have come into the spotlight and are seen today as prime examples of American folk art.

The question of the degree to which quilts have their roots in African culture occupies such authorities as Maude Wahlman and Eli Leon, who have each written books on the subject. Both contend that choices of pattern and color, particularly in pieces from the antebellum period, can be traced directly back to African aesthetic traditions.

When Wahlman and Leon examine patterns and motifs in African-American quilts, they see evidence of the cloth-weaving methods of West African societies. Wahlman cites the use of bold colors, large shapes, and asymmetrical configurations to support her theory that while many quilts "were done in the traditional Anglo-American styles," those intended "for personal, often utilitarian, uses by African-

Americans were designed and stitched with African traditions in mind." She believes that African-American quilters would take traditional European forms and Africanize them by manipulating patterns into unpredictable arrangements. These African retentions were unconscious, passing from one generation to the next without explanation of their sources.

Harriet Powers, who worked in the late nineteenth and early twentieth centuries, is known for only two pieces but is nevertheless a major figure in the history of American quilting. In her brilliantly pictorial and mysterious quilts, with their strange figures and baffling symbols, some see strong evidence of African cultural influences, while others see simply her membership, along with her husband, in the Masonic order or some other secret organization.

Cuesta Benberry, the author of *Always There: The African-American Presence in American Quilts,* is reluctant to try to pin down the influences that affected early African-American quilters. "When enigmatic symbols are encountered on early African-American quilts, a current tendency is to attribute them to an unconscious African cultural memory on the part of the quiltmaker. Nevertheless, this is only one of a number of avenues to explore."

Those relatively few quilts that can be definitely dated to the years before the Civil War were often made by highly skilled slaves, working under the direction of, and sometimes in collaboration with, plantation mistresses. Some spectacular quilts from that period came from the hands of free blacks, whose work was greatly prized by the local gentry.

The more African-American quilts become known, the more they will attract attempts to place them in a scholarly or art-historical framework. Benberry mentions stories suggesting that quilts were hung outside safe houses as markers for passengers on the Underground Railroad. Quilts made in the Jacob's Ladder pattern (later christened the Underground Railroad) may have originated in the Western Reserve region of Ohio and in western Kentucky, both frequent resting places for those escaping North.

Colors also play a role in quilt lore. One writer has speculated that a quilt containing black may also have announced an Underground Railroad station. Some think blue promised protection and success. Theories like these may or may not ever find proof, but in the end it is the quilts themselves that draw us. Some bear bold, outsize, vaguely human or vegetable shapes; others are veritable flower gardens pieced together with tiny, regular stitches; and still others play with the eye to form powerful and oddly modern optical illusions.

Even as the opposing theorists explore this uncharted territory, they find common ground, seeing in African-American quilts the blending of several cultures—African, Native American, and European—to form a creolized art with a distinctly American character. Today artists find inspiration in the quilts' beautiful simplicity. Romare Bearden spoke of looking at various quilt patterns as a child and later incorporating their pieced and overlapping textures into his collages. Present-day quilters often consciously use African-inspired imagery in their works, explicitly linking their art and lives to their ancestral heritage.

Whether my great-grandmother quilted with African aesthetic principles in mind I can only guess. I do know that she was a strong believer in what Toni Morrison calls "rootedness," recognizing that self-awareness and a strong sense of family history are important tools to get you through life. Now when I run my fingers over the surface of our quilts, I feel where she pulled the knots a little tighter in places and remember a woman whose face I see clearly only in Polaroids, but whose memories—preserved in scraps of old dresses, pants, and bed sheets—are inextricably stitched to mine.

Comprehension
1. Why are the family quilts so important to the writer?
   a. She believes that in the future they will be worth a lot of money.
   b. They remind her of individual members of her extended family.
   c. They symbolize the African quilting tradition.
   d. She enjoys showing them to her friends.

1. _____

Making Inferences
2. Which of the following statements would the writer probably disagree with?
   a. Many people are becoming interested in the origins and meanings of African American quilts.
   b. Experts disagree about the meanings of African American quilts and the inspiration for their designs.
   c. It is important to learn about your family and your cultural heritage.
   d. It is easy to trace the origin of the African American quilting tradition.

2. _____

Using Context Clues
3. In paragraph 9 the word *enigmatic* means
   a. puzzling
   b. beautiful
   c. old-fashioned
   d. well understood

3. _____

Distinguishing Fact from Opinion
4. According to the writer, which of the following statements is a fact rather than an opinion?
   a. Early African American quilters were undoubtedly inspired by African culture.
   b. Many modern quilters make deliberate use of designs inspired by African art.
   c. In many quilts the colors have a special, symbolic meaning.
   d. Quilters have always known that their products are works of art.

4. _____

Identifying the Main Idea

5. The main idea of the article is that
   a. self-awareness and a sense of family history are important tools for life
   b. African American folk art owes a great deal to its African heritage
   c. we cannot determine the degree to which African American quilts are inspired by African culture
   d. African American quilts are now considered a form of American folk art

5. _____

A Swimming Lesson (Memoir)
Jewelle L. Gomez

At nine years old I didn't realize my grandmother, Lydia, and I were doing an extraordinary thing by packing a picnic lunch and riding the elevated train from Roxbury to Revere Beach. It seemed part of the natural rhythm of summer to me. I didn't notice how the subway cars slowly emptied of most of their Black passengers as the train left Boston's urban center and made its way into the Italian and Irish suburban neighborhoods to the north. It didn't seem odd that all of the Black families stayed in one section of the beach and never ventured onto the boardwalk to the concession stands or the rides except in groups.

I do remember Black women perched cautiously on their blankets, tugging desperately at bathing suits rising too high and complaining about their hair "going back." Not my grandmother, though. She glowed with unashamed athleticism as she waded out, just inside the reach of the waves, and moved along the riptide parallel to the shore. Once submerged, she would load me onto her back and begin her long, tireless strokes. With the waves partially covering us, I followed her rhythm with my short, chubby arms, taking my cues from the powerful movement of her back muscles. We did this again and again until I'd fall off, and she'd catch me and set me upright in the strong New England surf. I was thrilled by the wildness of the ocean and my grandmother's fearless relationship to it. I loved the way she never consulted her mirror after her swim, but always looked as if she had been born to the sea, a kind of aquatic heiress.

None of the social issues of 1957 had a chance of catching my attention that year. All that existed for me was my grandmother, rising from the surf like a Dahomean queen, shaking her head free of her torturous rubber cap, beaming down at me when I finally took the first strokes on my own. She towered above me in the sun with a benevolence that made simply dwelling in her presence a reward in itself. Under her gaze I felt part of a long line of royalty. I was certain that everyone around us—Black and white—saw and respected her magnificence.

Although I sensed her power, I didn't know the real significance of our summers together as Black females in a white part of town. Unlike winter, when we were protected by the cover of coats, boots and hats, summer left us vulnerable and at odds with the expectations for women's bodies—the narrow hips, straight hair, flat stomachs, small feet—handed down from the mainstream culture and media. But Lydia never noticed. Her long chorus-girl legs ended in size-nine shoes, and she dared to make herself even bigger as she stretched her broad back and became a woman with a purpose: teaching her granddaughter to swim.

My swimming lessons may have seemed a superfluous skill to those who watched our lessons. After all, it was obvious that I wouldn't be doing the backstroke on the Riviera or in the pool of a penthouse spa. Certainly nothing in the popular media at that time made the "great outdoors" seem a hospitable place for Black people. But my prospects for utilizing my skill were irrelevant to me, and when I finally got it right I felt as if I had learned some invaluable life secret.

When I reached college and learned the specifics of slavery and the Middle Passage, the magnitude of that "peculiar institution" was almost beyond my comprehension; it was like nothing I'd learned before about the history of my people. It was difficult making a connection with those Africans who had been set adrift from their own land. My initial reaction was "Why didn't the slaves simply jump from the ships while they were still close to shore, and swim home?" The child in me who had learned to survive in water was crushed to find that my ancestors had not necessarily shared this skill. Years later when I visited West Africa and learned of the poisonous, spiny fish that inhabit most of the coastal waters, I understood why swimming was not the local sport there that it was in New England. And now when I take to the surf, I think of those ancestors and of Lydia.

The sea has been a fearful place for us. It swallowed us whole when there was no escape from the holds of slave ships. For me, to whom the dark fathoms of a tenement hallway were the most unknowable thing so far encountered in my nine years, the ocean was a mystery of terrifying proportions. In teaching me to swim, my grandmother took away my fear. I began to understand something outside myself—the sea—and consequently something about myself as well. I was no longer simply a fat little girl: My body had become a sea vessel—sturdy, enduring, graceful. I had the means to be safe.

Before she died last summer I learned that Lydia herself couldn't really swim that well. As I was splashing, desperately trying to learn the right rhythm—face down, eyes closed, air out, reach, face up, eyes open, air in, reach—Lydia was brushing the ocean's floor with her feet, keeping us both afloat. When she told me, I was stunned. I reached into my memory trying to combine this new information with the Olympic vision I'd always kept of her. At first I'd felt disappointed, tricked, the way I used to feel when I'd learn that a favorite movie star was only five feet tall. But then I quickly realized what an incredible act of bravery it was for her to pass on to me a skill she herself had not quite mastered—a skill that she knew would always bring me a sense of accomplishment. And it was more than just the swimming. It was the ability to stand on any beach anywhere and be proud of my large body, my African hair. It was not fearing the strong muscles in my own back; it was gaining control over my own life.

Now when the weather turns cold and I don the layers of wool and down that protect me from the eastern winters, I remember the power of my grandmother's broad back and I imagine I'm wearing my swimsuit. Face up, eyes open, air in, reach.

Making Inferences
6. What was the "real significance" of the grandmother's behavior at the beach?
   a. She demonstrated courage and a sense of pride in who she was.
   b. It was unusual for a woman her age to be able to swim so well.
   c. Others noticed what a strikingly beautiful woman she was.
   d. She was teaching her granddaughter about the history of their ancestors.　6. _____

Understanding Cause and Effect
7. Learning to swim had the effect of helping the writer
   a. develop self-confidence and a sense of control over her life
   b. better understand the issues involved in the struggle for civil rights
   c. develop a sense of humor
   d. appreciate the neighborhood in which she grew up　7. _____

Using Context Clues
8. In paragraph 5 the word *superfluous* means
   a. exciting
   b. difficult
   c. unnecessary
   d. amazing　8. _____

Distinguishing Fact from Opinion

9. Which of the following statements expresses an opinion rather than a fact?
    a. The writer's ancestors did not swim in the waters along the coast of West Africa.
    b. All who saw the writer's grandmother swimming felt admiration and respect for her.
    c. The writer's grandmother did not really swim very well.
    d. The writer paid little attention to the social issues of 1957.

9. _____

Understanding the Author's Point of View and Purpose

10. In this memoir, the author is trying to show
    a. that learning to swim can help a person develop self-esteem
    b. that her grandmother was a gifted teacher
    c. that it is okay to lie in order to teach someone something
    d. how her grandmother helped her develop self-confidence and gain control over her own life

10. _____

The Homeplace (Poem)
Lenard D. Moore

When I walk the path this morning
there is only a slight light
in the thinned woods.
I come upon a creek
near a tin-roofed house;   5
and there's no one anywhere
to witness my presence.

Meanwhile the wind
rises through the branches—
but soon reaches groundfall.   10
A faint smell of honeysuckle
sustains itself on the air
while quail rove the slope-weeds.
My eyes will not let go.

Now I think of my great-grandfather   15
who one time walked these woods through daylight.
This is the country he knew since boyhood.
And I am grateful for this homeplace—
here, I, too, wish to grow old
and stand without words   20
in this part of the world
so lively and pure.

I can hear a dog barking
somewhere in the far distance—
here where the voices of former life   25
do not speak, their spirits huddling
into themselves, a brotherhood of saints.
We are this fresh green world
which cradles everything into itself.

Making Inferences
11. The writer is grateful for the "homeplace" because
    a. the landscape there is beautiful
    b. it gives him a sense of connection with previous generations
    c. he was able to plant a garden there
    d. the land is part of his inheritance   11. _____

Understanding the Author's Point of View and Purpose
12. Which word best describes the speaker's tone as he describes his walk
    along the path?
    a. bitter   **b.** anxious   **c.** sorrowful   **d.** reflective   12. _____

Understanding Cause and Effect

13. Walking through the woods causes the speaker to think about
    a. how hard it had been for his family to survive
    b. how he wishes he lived in a more exciting part of the world
    c. the members of his family who had lived there before him
    d. the loneliness he feels standing there by himself   13. _____

Identifying the Main Idea

14. In this poem the author is saying that
    a. once you leave your home, you can never really go back again
    b. we should never forget the past
    c. he feels a connection with his ancestors
    d. as he grew up, he began to appreciate his family more   14. _____

Interpreting Poetry

15. "We are this fresh green world" on line 28 is an example of
    a. a simile
    b. personification
    c. a metaphor
    d. alliteration   15. _____

Questions 16–20 relate to "Family Fabrics," "A Swimming Lesson" and
"The Homeplace."

Comparing and Contrasting

16. What do the selections by Atiya Butler, Jewelle L. Gomez, and Lenard D.
    Moore have in common?
    a. They discuss the connection between traditional handicrafts and cultural
       heritage.
    b. They explain the importance of developing a sense of self-esteem.
    c. They contain descriptions of close family members.
    d. They contain reflections about family members who are important to them.   16. _____

17. Which statement about the selections by Butler and Gomez is true?
    a. Both describe a traditional skill that has been handed down from one
       generation to another.
    b. Both discuss the role of folk art in the preservation of cultural heritage.
    c. Both describe a strong sense of connection with a family member.
    d. Both show the importance of determination and perseverance in
       acquiring a skill.   17. _____

Making Inferences

18. Which of the following statements would Butler, Gomez, and Moore most
    likely agree with?
    a. It is important to learn to stand on your own two feet.
    b. We should all grow up to be like our parents and grandparents.
    c. The past contains many lessons for today.
    d. It is important to make some kind of connection with your ancestors.   18. _____

Understanding the Author's Point of View and Purpose

19. Which word best describes the attitude of Gomez and Moore toward the family members they are writing about?
    a. humor
    b. respect
    c. suspicion
    d. sarcasm   19. _____

Making Generalizations

20. The selections by Butler, Gomez, and Moore all make the point that
    a. our ancestors faced the same problems and struggles that we face today
    b. everyone should learn some type of skill
    c. members of our family, even those who are gone, can have an important effect on our lives
    d. it is not good to dwell on the past   20. _____

B. Writing a Response to the Readings

The focus question that precedes the selections on pages 175–181 asks how the bonds we have with members of our family can affect our lives. Read the following scenario and think about how it relates to the selections you have just read. You may discuss your ideas with a small group of classmates or a partner. Then respond to the scenario question in a well-planned essay.

Scenario

While cleaning out her grandfather's attic, Kira comes across a very old trunk that belonged to her great-grandfather. The trunk is filled with books, letters, and mementos from her great-grandfather's youth. Kira shows the trunk to her father, who thinks that the items in the trunk may be very valuable. He wants to have them appraised by an antiques dealer. By selling the trunk the family would have enough money to buy a video camera system.

Kira's mother is excited about the discovery of the trunk, and she is upset at the idea of selling it. She says the trunk is more valuable to the family than money and that they should keep it as a memento of family history.

Scenario Question

What should the family members do to resolve their differences?